Margaret Brown's French Cookery Book

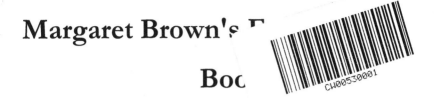

Margaret Brown

Alpha Editions

This edition published in 2022

ISBN : 9789356786660

Design and Setting By
Alpha Editions
www.alphaedis.com
Email - info@alphaedis.com

PREFACE.

This book contains a variety of receipts, from the finest French dishes to the most ordinary cooking. They are reliable, as nearly every one has been used by me at different times. My experience in the work has prompted me to issue this book, every part of which has been dictated by me, and carefully written down by my friend, Louise A. Smith.

MARGARET BROWN.

QUANTITY FOR A
RECEPTION OR EVENING PARTY
OF 225 PERSONS.

14 dozen Croquettes; 1 Boned Turkey; 8 quarts Terrapin.

(Six turkeys, 2½ chickens, 6 dozen stalks of celery, 6 heads of lettuce, 3 half-pint bottles of olive oil are required for chicken salad; 2½ dozen eggs for the dressing and garnishing. Parsley can also be used for garnishing the dishes.)

[This quantity can be increased or lessened in proportion to the above number.]

FOR A SPRING LUNCH.

Little Neck clams or deviled crabs; patties; spring chickens; squabs; pate de foie gras, or a bird glace; ices and fruits.

DINNER FOR 12 PERSONS.

Oysters (Blue Point), 5 or 6 on a plate; Julienne soup or puree of chicken or asparagus, followed by a course of fish; patties, either chicken or mushroom. For filet de bœuf, take 5 or 6 pounds fillet. In the spring garnish this dish with mushrooms, or asparagus and French potatoes; macaroni timbale; sweetbreads, larded and roasted, served with pease; supreme of chicken; salad and crushed chunks; cheese souffle; ices, fruits, coffee.

A SPRING BREAKFAST.

Oranges with scalloped peel; broiled fish cutlets and potato croquettes; lamb chops and pease (French chops); vol-au-vents of sweetbreads; broiled squabs; waffles and coffee; cheese, straws, ices.

MARGARET BROWN'S
FRENCH COOKERY BOOK.

No. 1.

OX TAIL SOUP.

Soak 3 tails in warm water. Put into a gallon stewpan 8 cloves, 2 onions, 1 teaspoonful each of allspice and black pepper, and the tails cover with cold water. Skim often and carefully. Let simmer gently until the meat is tender and leaves the bones easily. This will take 2 hours. When done take out the meat and cut it off the bones. Skim the broth and strain it through a sieve. To thicken it put in flour and butter, or 2 tablespoonfuls of the fat you have taken off the broth into a clean stewpan, with as much flour as will make a paste. Stir well over the fire; then pour in the broth slowly while stirring. Let it simmer for one-half hour; skim, and strain through a sieve. Put in the meat with a tablespoonful of mushroom catsup, a glass of wine; season with salt.

No. 2.

MOCK TURTLE.

Get a calf's head with skin on, take out the brains, wash the head several times in cold water, let it soak one hour in spring water, then lay in a stewpan, and cover with cold water, and half a gallon over. Take off the scum that rises as it warms. Let it boil for one hour, take it up and, when almost cold, cut the head into pieces one and a half inches, and the tongue into mouthfuls, or make a side dish of tongue and brains. When the head is taken out put in the stock meat, about 3 pounds of knuckle of veal, and as much beef, add all the trimmings and bones of the head, skim it well, cover close, let it boil 5 hours (save 2 quarts of this for gravy sauce), strain it off and let stand until morning; then take off the fat; set a large stewpan on the fire, with half a pound of fresh butter, 12 ounces of sliced onions, 4 ounces of green sage; chop it a little; let these fry 1 hour, then rub in one pound of flour, then add the broth by degrees until it is as thick as cream. Season with ¼ ounce of ground allspice, ½ ounce of black pepper ground fine, salt to your taste the rind of a lemon peeled thin. Let it simmer gently for 1½ hours, strain through a hair sieve. If it does not go through easily press a wooden spoon against the sides of the sieve. Put it in a clean stewpan with the head, and season it by putting to each gallon of soup ½ pint of wine, 2 tablespoonfuls of lemon juice. Let it simmer until the meat is tender (from ½ hour to 1 hour). Take care it is not overdone. Stir often to keep the meat from sticking to the pan. When the meat is quite tender the soup is ready. A head of 20 pounds and 10 pounds of stock-meat will make 10 quarts soup, besides the 2 quarts of stock-meat set aside for side dishes. If there is more meat on the head than you wish to use make a ragout pie of some of it.

No. 3.

MOCK MOCK TURTLE.

Line the bottom of a 5-pint stewpan with 1 ounce of lean bacon or ham, 1½ pounds lean gravy beef, a cow's heel, inner rind of a carrot, a sprig of lemon thyme, winter savory, 3 sprigs of parsley, a few green leaves of sweet basil, 2 onions, a large onion with 4 cloves stuck in it, 18 grains of allspice, 18 grains of pepper. Pour on these 1 pint of cold water, cover the stewpan and set it on a slow fire to boil gently ¼ hour. Watch it carefully, if need be, with the cover off, until it gets a good brown color; then fill up the stewpan with boiling water, and let it simmer for 2 hours. If you wish you can cut up some of the meat into mouthfuls and put into the soup. To thicken it take 2 tablespoonfuls of flour, a ladleful of gravy, mix them and pour it into the stewpan where the gravy is, let it simmer ½ hour longer. Skim it and strain through a fine sieve. Cut the cow's heel in pieces 1 inch square. Squeeze the juice of a lemon, 1 tablespoonful of mushroom catsup, 1 teaspoonful of salt, ½ teaspoonful of black pepper, a pinch of grated nutmeg, a glass of Madeira or sherry wine, through a sieve into the stewpan of soup; let simmer 5 minutes longer.

No. 4.

SOUTHERN MOCK TURTLE SOUP.

Wash a calf's head clean, put 2 gallons of water on it, set it to boil; put in a hock of ham (smoked), weighing about 2 pounds, also thyme, 3 onions, 1 bunch of celery tops, 1 tablespoonful each of allspice cloves, not ground; let it boil down slowly to 1½ gallons. When the head is done take it out, being careful to remove the brains and tongue, then cut the meat into small pieces. Strain the soup; brown ½ pound of flour and make a batter of it to thicken the soup; grate ½ of a nutmeg in it, put in pepper and salt to taste; take a portion of the brain and make it into small cakes, as you would fritters, fry them in lard; take ½ pound of veal cutlets, and a small part of the ham, chop up with a little parsley and onion, season with pepper and salt; make small forcemeat balls, frying them in lard, having first rolled them in eggs, then in breadcrumbs; put the forcemeat ball in the soup just before dishing up, together with ½ pint of wine.

CELERY SOUP.

After splitting 6 heads of celery into pieces about 2 inches long, wash them well, lay them on a hair sieve to drain, and put them in 3 quarts of clear gravy soup in a gallon soup-pot; let it stew just enough to make the celery tender, say about 1 hour; take off the scum if any should rise, season with a little salt. Should you wish to make this soup at a season when you could not get celery, use the celery seed, say about ½ pint, put this in the soup ¼ hour before it is done, with a little sugar.

No. 6.

PEASE SOUP AND PICKLED PORK.

Take 2 pounds of the flank of pickled pork. Care must be taken that the pork is not too salty, otherwise lay it in water the night before. Put 1 quart pease (split), 2 heads of cut celery, 2 onions peeled, 1 sprig of sweet marjoram in 3 quarts of water; boil gently for 2 hours, then put in the pork. Let this boil until it is done enough to eat. When done wash it clean in hot water and place it on a dish, or else cut it in mouthfuls and put in a tureen with the soup.

No. 7.

PLAIN PEASE SOUP.

One quart of split peas, 2 heads of celery; let them simmer gently in broth or soft water (3 quarts) over a slow fire, stirring every now and then to keep the pease from burning. Add more water should it boil away or the soup get too thick. After boiling for 3 hours put them through a coarse sieve, then through a fine one. Wash out your stewpan and put the soup back into it, let it boil up once. Take off the scum if any. Fry small square pieces of bread in hot lard until they become a delicate brown; take them out and let them drain on a sheet of paper. Send these up with the soup in one side dish and dry powdered mint or sweet marjoram in another.

No. 8.

LOBSTER SOUP.

Take 3 fine, lively hen lobsters, boil them; when cold split the tails; take out the fish, crack the claws, and cut the meat in mouthfuls; take out the coral and soft part of the body, crush part of the coral in a mortar; pick out the fish from the shell, beat part of it with the coral; out of this make forcemeat balls, flavored with mace, nutmeg, grated lemon peel, cayenne, and anchovy. Pound these, with the yolk of an egg. Have ready 3 quarts of veal broth, bruise the small legs and the shell, and put them into it to boil for 20 minutes, then strain. To thicken the soup take the live spawn, crush it in the mortar, with a little butter and flour, rub it through a sieve and add it to the soup with the meat of the lobsters and the rest of the coral; let it simmer gently for 10 minutes.

No. 9.

ASPARAGUS SOUP.

Take all the tender portion of three good-sized bunches of asparagus. This will make 2 quarts of soup. Put a large saucepan half full of water on the fire; when it boils put one-half of the asparagus in, with a little salt; let it boil till done, then drain it off. Put in a clean stewpan, with 3 quarts of plain veal or mutton broth, cover up close, and stew one hour over a slow fire. Rub through a sieve, then cut the other half of the asparagus in pieces one inch long, and send up in the soup.

No. 10.

TOMATO SOUP OR MOCK HOCK SOUP.

One quart of tomatoes, put on fire and let boil; when done mash through a sieve 3 tablespoonfuls of sugar, 1 teaspoonful nutmeg and mace together, and put in tomatoes, 1 tablespoonful of butter, mixed with a large tablespoonful of flour, stir all into the tomatoes, and put on to boil again; stir till it boils. Quarter of an hour before serving pour in 1 pint of milk. Pepper and salt to taste. Stir till it boils up nicely. Put in 2 tablespoonfuls wine just before dishing up.

No. 11.

FRIED OYSTERS.

For this purpose each and every oyster should be as large, plump, and fat—fresh, of course, not salt—as you can procure. Any small ones will serve for sauces, croquettes, soups, etc. Drain off their juice, put them in a bowl, cover them with ice water, let stand a few minutes, then place them in a colander and drain them. Dry between two thin, soft towels, without pressing them, and lay upon a moulding-board, slightly coated with cracker-dust, finely sifted. Beat up to a thick rich custard as many eggs and an equal measure of cream as you need for moistening all the oysters, adding, at the last, a saltspoonful of salt for every three eggs. Have ready a sufficiency of finely-sifted bread crumbs prepared by rubbing the heart of a stale loaf of white bread in a towel and pressing it through a sieve. Dip the oysters, one by one, into the beaten egg and roll them in the crumbs till covered in every part. By no means flatten them, but keep them as round and plump as possible; lay them on napkins and keep in a cool place for half an hour; again dip, roll in crumbs, and set aside for another half hour. Now lay them on the wire stand, not quite touching each other. Set the stand into a deep frying-pan nearly full of whatever frying mixture you use, which must be boiling hot, and fry quickly to a deep yellow color, but do not brown them, or they will be tough and greasy. Lift the stand out of the pan, drain quickly, and serve the oysters on a hot, white napkin, placed on a hot platter, and garnish with sprigs of parsley or water cress, stuffed olives, and small bits of lemon. The daintiest condiment of all is the French mayonnaise sauce served with lettuce.

No. 12.

FRICASSEED OYSTERS.

Fifty oysters, 6 ounces butter, 3 tablespoonfuls flour, 3 saltspoonfuls salt, 2 saltspoonfuls white pepper, 2 saltspoonfuls mace, 6 bay leaves, 1 quart cream, 4 yolks of eggs, 1 tea cupful bread crumbs. Put the oysters, with their juice, into a stewpan on a quick fire; give one boil, drain them, put them into a hot tureen, and set in a warm place. Rub the butter, flour, and 3 teaspoonfuls of scalding cream to a fine smooth paste, stir it quickly into the quart of cream in a bright stewpan on a quick fire. Add the salt and spice, and stir till it no longer thickens. Now put in the yolks of eggs, well beaten; stir till smooth, strain the whole through a fine sieve upon the oysters. Cover evenly with the crumbs and lightly brown in a quick oven.

No. 13.

SCALLOPED OYSTERS.

Half-gallon oysters for a three pint pudding dish; drain the oysters well, 1 pint of bread-crumbs, and put pepper, salt, and a little mustard, nutmeg or mace in the crumbs. Cover the bottom of dish with the crumbs. Put a layer of oysters with a small piece of butter, then a layer of crumbs. Continue this way till dish is full, then put 2 or 3 tablespoonfuls of cream on top. Put in a rather quick oven; let bake 20 minutes.

No. 14.

PICKLED OYSTERS.

Drain the oysters. To ½ gallon of pickled oysters, ½ pint cider vinegar. Heat the vinegar boiling hot. Put in spice enough to flavor, cloves, allspice and mace. Put the oysters in the hot liquor till they get hot; put a little salt in them; scoop them out of the hot liquor and put them right into the hot vinegar, and put in a covered dish and set away to cool.

No. 15.

FRICASSEE OF OYSTERS.

Set 75 oysters on the fire with their liquor and an equal quantity of chicken broth, 1 glass white wine, 2 blades mace; when they boil remove from the fire, and then from the boiling braise, which return to the fire; in a clean stewpan put a piece of butter the size of an egg, 1½ teaspoonfuls of flour, stir 5 minutes then add the yolks of 5 eggs, 1 saltspoonful of white pepper and salt, 1 tablespoonful chopped parsley; don't let it boil; make the oysters hot in it; use as directed.

No. 16.

CHICKEN A L'ITALIENNE.

Common butter, remains of chicken, 12 tomatoes, 1 cup broth, 2 tablespoonfuls onions chopped, a tablespoonful parsley, 1 saltspoonful each of salt, white pepper, royal thyme, and summer savory, 1 tablespoonful of butter. Cut the remains of chicken into small pieces, dip into the butter, and fry crisp in plenty of lard made hot for the purpose; serve with tomato sauce.

No. 17.

FISH CROQUETTES.

Three-pound rock. Boil it till done; skin it and take bones out. Chop fish up fine with 1 stalk of celery and 2 sprigs of parsley, 1 pint milk, 2 tablespoonfuls flour, ¼ pound butter. Mix butter and flour together; boil the milk and pour it into the flour and butter, making a rich sauce. Boil ½ pint oysters scalded, take the hearts out, cut them up in small bits and put in the sauce. Put fish in the sauce and keep stirring till it begins to boil. When done pour out on a platter and let it get cold. Make croquettes in shape of pears or apples, roll in beaten eggs and then in bread crumbs. Boil in a croquette kettle of lard.

Serve these with French potatoes or Saratoga potatoes fried.

No. 18.

POTATO CROQUETTES.

Peel and boil 5 good-sized potatoes till mealy. Rub them fine with a potato-masher; ½ tablespoonful butter, 2 eggs, pepper and salt mashed well in the potatoes. After they are cool make them out into steeples. Roll them in beaten egg, then in bread crumbs; boil them in hot lard. Set them up around the dish.

No. 19.

LOBSTER CROQUETTES.

Two lobsters boiled done, picked and chopped fine; ¼ loaf of bread grated fine, little nutmeg, mace to taste, ¼ pound of butter; mix all with lobster and 1 egg; make lobster croquettes in pears or steeples, put them in beaten eggs, then in bread crumbs. Boil in hot lard, garnish with the claws and parsley.

No. 20.

WINE SAUCE FOR VENISON OR HARE.

Quarter pint of claret or port wine, and same quantity of plain mutton gravy; 1 tablespoonful currant jelly. Let boil up once and send to table in a sauce-boat.

No. 21.

MARROW BONES.

Saw the bones even so they will stand steadily; put a piece of paste into the ends, set them upright in a saucepan, and boil till done. A beef-marrow bone will take from 1 hour to 1½ hours. Serve fresh toasted bread with them.

No. 22.

CURRY CHICKEN.

Two young chickens, cut up in joints; place in stewpan a small piece of butter, a little piece of onion and parsley, 1 pint of water. Let stew slowly. When most done take 1 teacup of cream, take grease off the top of the pot, pour in the cream; take the grease, mix it with 2 large tablespoonfuls of flour; when the chicken begins to boil again put in the flour moistened with the grease; put in a teaspoonful of curry and a little salt. Boil some plain rice in a stewpan, when time to dish up put the curry chicken in center of platter, and the boiled rice all around the dish, and garnish with water-cresses and parsley.

No. 23.

COLD VEAL AND HAM TIMBALE.

Timbale paste, 1 pound corned ham, 2 pounds leg veal, 6 hard boiled eggs, 1 teaspoonful each of royal celery, salt, and marjoram, 3 sprigs parsley, white pepper, and salt to taste. Line the timbale mould with the paste, first setting it on a greased baking pan; cut the ham and veal into scallops, and the eggs into slices; with them make alternate layers with the seasonings; when all are used, fill with water, wet the exposed edges, and bake in moderate oven 2 hours; when cold open the mould, and serve as may be desired.

No. 24.

RISSOLES OF CHICKENS.

CHROMSKY MIXTURE.

Roll out paste very thin, cut out with large biscuit cutter, wet the edges, put a teaspoonful of the mixture on, fold the paste over it pressing the two edges; fry in plenty of lard made hot for the purpose, until the paste is cooked. Serve on a napkin.

No. 25.

TERRAPIN.

Take 2 diamond-backs, put them into hot, boiling water or lye. Let them get entirely done; take them out and let them get cool a little; then open them and take the dark skin off the feet; take out the meat from the shell, the entrails, and the liver, being careful not to break the gall, as it will render the dish unfit to eat; do not use the head; take ¼ pound of butter, a small piece of onion, teaspoonful of thyme. Put these in the stewpan and let them get a little brown, putting in also a tablespoonful of flour, ½ pint of cream, and ½ pint of milk. Let all this boil to a rich sauce, then take it off the fire; grate a little nutmeg, a pinch of ground allspice and cloves, cayenne pepper to taste. Take one stalk of celery and chop it up very fine; put it with the meat; put this in the stewpan of sauce ¼ hour before dinner on a fire; let it boil up for 5 or 10 minutes. Just before dishing up put in a wineglass each of sherry and brandy. Sliders can be cooked in the same way.

ROAST BONED TURKEY.

This must be boned, as stated in Boned Turkey, with this exception: The bones must be left in all the lower extremities and in the pinions, so that when placed in shape these bones will help to form it. Take a stale loaf of bread, cut all the crust off; ½ pound of butter, 1 can of mushrooms, chopped, pepper and salt, 1 teaspoonful of nutmeg. Chop all this up fine; stuff every joint where the bone has been taken out so that it will look plump; tie it up; put in a baking-pan; sift flour, pepper and salt over it; place a little water in the pan to keep it from burning; bake 1½ hours in a slow oven; baste it with ½ pint of Madeira wine in the oven; take the turkey out of the pan and make the gravy with the essence. Make potato croquettes and set all around the dish.

No. 27.

BONED TURKEY.

Split the turkey down the back, clear the back of meat, then take all the meat off the wings without breaking the skin, then from the side of the breast, afterwards from the thighs and legs. We have now taken all the meat off in one piece, leaving only the carcass of bones. Now take 2 pounds veal-cutlet, or large-sized chicken, or sausage-meat, ¼ pound ham, a half-sized can truffles peeled and sliced in half, a can of mushrooms sliced in half, 1 large stalk celery, 1 teaspoonful thyme, a half of a small onion, a bunch of parsley; chop fine, except the truffles and mushrooms; season with pepper and salt to taste. Take all the dressing together and put it in the meat (which is all in one piece) taken off the turkey; sew the back up; then sew this in a bag, and boil gently. A small-sized turkey will take 2½ hours; a large-sized, 3 hours. Place the carcass in ½ gallon of water and let boil till water is reduced to 3 pints; put in it pepper and salt and a small piece of onion; then take off and strain. Melt 1 box of gelatine in a cupful of water. When melted, put in the cool soup, with the whites of 2 beaten eggs and 2 egg shells. Put it on the fire and stir till it boils. Let boil 10 minutes, then strain through a flannel bag. Take a small mould of jelly, garnish with eggs, parsley, beets, and carrots, putting the jelly alternately between each till mould is filled. When the turkey is done put it in a close pan and press it. After getting perfectly cool, jelly with cool jelly, just cool enough to spread until the turkey is entirely covered. Put the garnishing moulds on the breast of turkey. Garnish dish with watercress, beets, and carrots.

No. 28.

CUSTARD FRITTERS.

Half pint milk, 5 eggs, ½ cupful of sugar, 1 gill of cream, common butter. Beat the milk, cream, sugar, and eggs together; strain, put into a small bowl, set in saucepan with boiling water to reach half way up the sides of the bowl; steam very gently until set—about 20 minutes—place on the ice until cold; cut into pieces 1½ inches long by 1 square; dip into common batter, and fry in plenty of hot lard, a deep fawn color. Serve sprinkled with sugar.

No. 29.

PEACH SAUCE.

Place the peach juice from the can into a small saucepan, add an equal volume of water, a little more sugar, and 8 or 10 raisins, boil this 10 minutes, strain, and just before serving add 8 drops of extract of bitter almonds.

No. 30.

LOBSTER FRITTERS.

Common batter, 1 lobster, ½ cupful mushrooms, yolks of 4 eggs, 1 cupful of cream, 1 tablespoonful of butter, celery, salt, thyme, white pepper, saltspoonful of parsley, and 1 tablespoonful of flour. Put the lobster in 2 quarts of boiling water, with ½ cupful salt; boil 25 minutes; when cold remove the meat and fat; cut into small neat slices; put the flour and butter on the fire in a small stewpan, stir with a wooden spoon until it bubbles, then add the cream boiling, and the seasoning; let it boil two minutes, add the yolks and lobster, and mix; set it back to simmer 4 minutes; pour it out on a well greased dish, and set it away to get firm by cooling; then cut into neat pieces, dip in batter, and fry yellow in plenty of lard made hot for the purpose; have a few nice branches of parsley, quite dry, and fry in the lard just while you count 15 seconds. Serve on the fritters.

No. 31.

BELL FRITTERS.

Sift 1 pint of flour, pour boiling-hot water on it until it cooks enough to have the consistency of a stiff batter. Let it get perfectly cold. Take 5 eggs, 1 tablespoonful of butter, and put in it and beat all up till it is as light as muffins. Grate in a little nutmeg. Boil them in hot lard. Make wine sauce to serve with them.

No. 32.

WAFFLES.

With yeast make a thick batter over night. In the morning stir in 1 pint of flour, 3 eggs, 1 tablespoonful of butter, and a little nutmeg and salt; let it raise again, and fry just before breakfast.

No. 33.

OMELETTE.

Five yolks of eggs, beaten light, and a little finely chopped celery. Beat the whites to a stiff froth. Just before breakfast put in a ¼ cup of milk, then pour the whites in with the yolks. Put in a buttered frying-pan and fry.

No. 34.

RAGOUT OF COLD VEAL.

The neck, loin, or fillet of veal can be used. Cut the veal in cutlets. Put in frying-pan a piece of butter; when hot, flour and fry the veal a light brown. Take it out, and put 1 pint of boiling water in the pan; give it a boil up for a minute and strain it into a basin, while you make a thickening as follows: Melt an ounce of butter in a pan and mix with it as much flour as will dry it up; stir it over the fire a few minutes and gradually add to it the gravy you made in the frying-pan; let them simmer together for ten minutes. Season with pepper, salt, a little mace, 1 wine-glass of mushroom catsup or wine till the meat is thoroughly warmed. Ready-boiled bacon, sliced, may be put in to warm with the veal.

No. 35.

LARK PIE.

Pick clean 4 dozen larks, singe them; cut off the wings and legs, take out the gizzards and place the larks on a dish. Cut 2 pounds veal cutlets and 1 pound of ham into scallops. Fry these in a pan with a little fresh butter, 1 can of mushrooms, some parsley, 1 small onion, half a bay leaf, 1 sprig of thyme chopped fine; season with cayenne and salt and the juice of lemon. To these add ¼ pint of mushroom catsup and the same quantity of rich gravy. Boil the whole for 3 minutes, then place the veal and ham scallops, one upon the other, in the bottom of the dish; put the larks neatly and closely to each other; upon them pour over the sauce, and put mushrooms in the centre. Cover with puff-paste. Bake pie 1¼ hours and serve.

CHICKEN PIE A LA REINE.

Paste, 1 plump tender chicken, ½ pound salt pork, ½ teaspoonful each of celery, salt, and thyme, 4 sprigs parsley, white pepper and salt to taste. Cut the chicken up in small joints, the pork in neat scallops, and stew gently in 1½ pints water until nearly cooked. Line the edge of a pudding dish with the paste, make layers of the chicken, pork, and seasonings; when used sprinkle over the chopped parsley; fill with the gravy, cover, ornament, and wash over with milk, and bake in steady oven 40 minutes.

No. 37.

LEMON CREAM MERINGUE PIE.

Having made the lemon cream pie, whip the 4 whites of eggs to a dry froth; gently incorporate 1 cupful sugar; spread over the top of the pie, and return to the oven to set; a fawn color.

No. 38.

TIMBALES OF MACARONI.

Take 2 quarts of water and boil 1 pound macaroni in it with ½ pound butter, 8 pepper-corns, and a little salt. When done and cold, let one-half of it drain upon a napkin. Butter the inside of a plain mould, cut the macaroni into half-inch lengths, and cover the bottom of the mould with these, placing them on end; cover this with a thick layer of chicken forcemeat; line the sides of the mould in the same way, smoothing the inside with the back of the spoon in hot water; fill the cavity with a blanquette of fowl which has a thick sauce; cover the whole with a layer of forcemeat as follows: Cut paper to fit the mould, butter it, spread some forcemeat on it, dip a knife in hot water and smooth the surface with it, take hold of the paper with both hands and turn it upside down upon the timbale. Leave the paper on in such a way that it can be easily removed when the forcemeat has steamed enough. One and a half hours before dinner place the timbale in a stewpan twice its size, upon a ring, to prevent it from touching the bottom, so that the water in the stewpan which only reaches half-way up the mould, may circulate freely under it. Place on the stove for an hour, then for ½ hour more put inside oven to let it get brown on top. When done, remove paper from the timbale, and carefully lift the mould. Pour some supreme sauce over it, and garnish with truffles and mushrooms.

No. 39.

SADDLE OF MUTTON.

Take a saddle of mutton, extract the spine bone carefully, trim the tail end round, cut the flaps square, season the inner part with pepper and salt, rolling up each flap so as to give a neat appearance, tying a string around it several times. The mutton must be prepared for braizing with carrots, onions, celery, cloves and mace; moisten with a quantity of good stock so as to cover the mutton; place a buttered paper and lid over all and set the braizing-pan on a moderate fire. After boiling let it continue to braize or simmer for 4 hours, carefully basting it; when done take it up and place in oven to dry on a pan. Dish it up and garnish with carrots, turnips, cauliflowers, French beans, cucumbers, asparagus heads, small new potatoes and green pease. Pour some sauce around the mutton and send to the table.

No. 40.

OX-TONGUE.

Get a pickled tongue, run an iron skewer through from one end to the other, tie a string from one end of skewer to the other, so as to make it keep its shape; put the tongue on the fire in cold water; let it boil gently for three hours, then take up, and after removing the outward cuticle or skin, place in larder to cool; trim neatly, wrap in a piece of buttered paper, put it in an oval stewpan with a little broth; ¾ of an hour before sending to table, put the tongue in oven or on slow fire to get warmed through, then glaze it and dish it up with some prepared spinach round it; pour a little sauce and serve.

No. 41.

MUTTON CUTLETS.

Trim the cutlets and arrange in circular order in a pan with a little clarified butter; fry quickly so as to brown on both sides; before quite done pour off the grease; add ½ pint of red wine (port or claret), 1 can prepared mushrooms and same quantity small onions previously simmered in a little butter over a slow fire till done; season with a pinch of mignonette pepper, little salt, some grated nutmeg, a teaspoonful pounded sugar; set the whole to boil on fire 2 minutes, add a spoonful of burnt sugar; allow the cutlets to simmer very slowly for 20 minutes. The cutlets must be dished up closely in a circle; add a half glass of red wine; boil the whole for 1 minute and garnish the center with mushrooms; pour the sauce over the cutlets and serve.

No. 42.

MUTTON CUTLETS WITH CHESTNUTS.

Dish up cutlets, as previously shown, garnish with chestnuts which have been equally heated in a stewpan, so that the husk will easily peel off; take the chestnuts with a little good broth and put in clean stewpan; let simmer; when done pound in a mortar; put in a pan with a little sugar, nutmeg, ½ pint of cream; reduce the pulp, rub through a sieve, put in stewpan, let it get hot, mix in some butter, pour round cutlets some thin sauce.

No. 43.

VOL-AU-VENTS.

[Quantity for 2 vol-au-vents].

Paste—One pound of butter, 1 pound of flour; divide butter in 4 parts, rub ¼ in flour, mix with hand, with a little water, then put on pastry board; roll out and put the second ¼ of butter in layers over this paste; fold and roll it, and add the other two quarters in the same way; keep 1 hour on ice to cool; roll and cut this paste in 4 parts; roll ¼ for the top and ¼ for the bottom of pie. These must be cut out oval shape; cut the pieces and ends left of the paste into flower shapes and leaves to garnish the sides of the 2 layers of pie. The remaining 2 quarters are for another vol-au-vent fixed in the same way. Cut out the center of top cover and fill in with flowers and leaves made of pastry. Put in a hot oven and let it bake ¾ of an hour. While baking this paste will rise and puff out in form like a cylinder. While hot take off this flowered center-piece on top of the pie, and from this opening scrape out all the insides, leaving nothing but a hollow cylinder of crust. Put in ½ dozen real sweetbreads, parboiled and skinned; 1 dozen truffles, peeled and sliced; ½ can of mushrooms cut in half. Make a sauce of 1 tablespoonful of butter, 1 of flour, ½ pint of cream, 1 pint milk; rub butter and flour together, boil milk and cream, and make a rich sauce of butter and flour, milk and cream, all mixed together; cook in this sauce sweetbreads, truffles, mushrooms, ½ teaspoonful of nutmeg, white pepper and salt each 1 teaspoonful; put in together; stir while boiling; boil 20 minutes. When ready for dinner fill up paste and serve with truffles, mushrooms, and sweetbreads while hot. Send sauce-boat full of sauce to the table with the paste.

No. 44.

CROQUETTES.

Take a medium-sized chicken, boil it, a pair of sweetbreads, and ½ box of mushrooms, 1 small can of truffles, 1 stalk of celery, a small onion, a few sprigs of parsley; chop all very fine; bring to a boil a sauce made of 1 pint of milk and chicken water ½ pint, a large tablespoonful of butter, 2 tablespoonfuls of flour, then beat 2 eggs in the sauce after cooling; season to taste with pepper, salt, and nutmeg; add the chopped chicken; put on to boil and stir 15 minutes; pour into platters to cool; then roll in the shape of pears or eggs; roll them in a beaten egg and then in bread crumbs; stick in a rib bone at the end of the pear shapes; boil them in hot lard a delicate brown; then lay on a napkin in a platter and garnish with parsley. Set them up on a dish in oval form.

No. 45.

ROCK-FISH CUTLET.

[Can be made from any fish.]

Take a rock-fish, after washing it clean cut it down the back-bone, take out the back-bone, cut the ribs off, then cut the fish in square pieces. Take the skin off of them, lard them with small pieces of truffles, which have been skinned and sliced, the slices being cut in three-quarters. Then take a sharp-pointed knife and thrust them into the fish. Salt the fish and put in a cool place for 1 hour. A half hour before dinner take a medium-sized dripping-pan, put in ½ pint of milk and a tablespoonful of butter; lay all the pieces of fish separate in this pan with the truffle side up, put a press on them to keep them straight, set on top of stove for ¼ hour. When done, take ½ pint milk, together with what milk is in the pan, 2 tablespoonfuls of flour, 1 teaspoonful of white pepper, 1 tablespoonful of butter; mix the butter and flour together till they come to a cream, then pour the hot milk on to make rich sauce. Put in this sauce 1 dozen mushrooms and what truffles are left; cut mushrooms in four quarters. Take up fish and lap it around your dish. Boil French potatoes and put them in the centre of dish; garnish the dish with parsley and sliced lemon.

No. 46.

RISSOLES.

Puff paste—Chop the breast of a chicken same as making croquettes. After boiling it take out 2 teaspoonfuls of the mixture, then roll the paste out very thin; take a biscuit-cutter and cut the paste; take the 2 teaspoonfuls of chicken-mixture and a beaten egg and wet the edge of the cut paste, also wet it all over the top, and roll them in vermicelli. Boil them till brown in hot lard. Serve on a napkin laid on a dish garnished with water-cresses.

[See receipt for making croquettes.]

No. 47.

CHICKEN CUTLETS.

[Quantity for one chicken.]

Boil the chicken sufficiently to eat; take it out and let it get cold; take all the white meat and chop up very fine with mushrooms and a celery stalk; take ¼ pound of butter, 2 full tablespoonfuls of flour, 2 yolks and 1 white of eggs, ½ pint of milk, ½ teacup of mushroom water, into which a little nutmeg has been grated, ½ pint of cream. Mix the butter and flour together, boil the milk and cream and mushroom water, into which put the butter and flour; this will make a rich sauce, which is seasoned to taste. When cooled a little add the beaten eggs; add chicken, stir up, making a rich paste; boil 15 minutes, stir while boiling, pour out in a platter, let get cold; make in shape of mutton cutlets or chops, take the ribs and put in for stems; then roll cutlets in beaten egg into which bread has been grated, put into hot lard and fry a delicate brown. Garnish with French pease and parsley, or mushrooms and parsley. Serve hot.

No. 48.

PATE-LA-FOIE-GRAS.

Make a soup of strong bouillon; let it boil for two hours; put in a few sprigs of thyme, one of onion, and a small bunch of celery tops; when done, let cool, and skim grease off. To every ½ pint jar of Pate-la-foie-gras, mix three pints of boullion; take a half box of gelatine melted in a teacup of bouillon; beat the white of one egg, and 2 egg-shells (not very light) in bouillon while cool, stir the melted gelatine till it begins to boil, say for about 10 minutes, add the pepper and salt. After boiling about 10 minutes strain through a flannel bag; put on ice, but do not let it get very cold. Put in a jelly mould a layer of jelly, cut mushrooms into stars and half-moons and lay on the layer of jelly, then a slice of Pate-la-foie-gras, next a layer of jelly, cut truffles into small pieces in the shape of flowers or diamonds, and lay on the layers of jelly; continue till the mould is filled, then put on ice; garnish to fancy.

No. 49.

CHICKEN SALAD WITH MAYONNAISE SAUCE.

One pair of chickens, boil them done; let get cold, skin them, and cut up in small dices; 2 dozen stalks of celery; cut up 4 white heads of lettuce, medium size; 1 of the white hard heads must be cut up with the celery and chicken. Take a teacupful of sweet oil, ¼ teacupful of vinegar, a light half teaspoonful of red pepper, salt to taste, 1 teaspoonful of mustard, 1 medium-sized tablespoonful Worcestershire sauce; mix that all up together with the chicken and celery; let the celery be perfectly dry. Take a medium-sized Irish potato, boil it done, squeeze it through a fine sieve; put in it a teaspoonful of mustard, cayenne pepper to taste, 2 yolks of raw eggs and 2 boiled ones mashed up very fine. Now beat the potatoes and eggs well up together, add half teacupful of vinegar, a little at a time, and the contents of 3 half pints of olive oil; work it one way till it becomes perfectly stiff and light; put it in ice-box 1 hour and let get cold. When you dish up put salad on dish, put the sweet oil dressing all over the top as an icing. Boil red beets and carrots, cut them into diamonds, roses, etc., and garnish the salad with it and sprigs of parsley; take the other three heads of lettuce, cut in four quarters, take one-quarter and put in center of salad, and put the others around the dish with parsley.

<h3 style="text-align:center">No. 50.</h3>

<h2 style="text-align:center">APPLE CHARLOTTE.</h2>

Take 6 large apples and chop very fine, grate the inside of a stale loaf of bread into crumbs, grate half a nutmeg, take a three-pint tin pudding-pan, line it thickly with thin-sliced buttered bread, a layer of bread crumbs, a layer of apples, and a layer of butter, composed of small pieces; continue to add till the pan is packed very tight—make the last layer of butter and sugar. Bake in a moderately hot oven two hours; serve with cream sauce. Put sugar in every layer.

<h3 style="text-align:center">No. 51.</h3>

<h2 style="text-align:center">CONSUMME.</h2>

Take a pint of consommé, with 3 well-beaten eggs in it, and a little salt, and pour it into a baking dish; put it in oven and let it bake 15 minutes. This will bake brown like a cake. Try with a knife-blade; if done the knife will be clear. Put it to cool, and then take the top and bottom crust off, cut the middle into diamonds and put them in tureen, and then pour over them the soup.

<h3 style="text-align:center">No. 52.</h3>

<h2 style="text-align:center">FISH CREAM A LA LAIT.</h2>

Take any kind of large white fish, 4 pounds to a three-pint pudding-pan; wash the fish in cold water, put on to boil, and let get cool. Take off the skin and flake the meat off the bones with a fork; parboil a pint of oysters; when done put to cool, then take out the hearts; boil half pint of milk and half pint of cream, beat up 2 tablespoonfuls of flour and 1 of butter to a light cream, which must be stirred into the boiling milk and cream; this will make a rich sauce; season with pepper and salt to taste. Take off the sauce when done and stir in fish and oysters, then put in a pudding-dish and put a layer of bread crumbs on top; over the bread crumbs put flakes of butter. Put in oven and let bake 20 minutes; make potato croquettes and lay on the dish, which must be garnished with parsley; serve hot.

No. 53.

SALMON FILLETS.

Take 5 pounds of salmon, cut it down the back, and take out the fillets. Lard it very close with thin strips of lard, put on with larding-needle. Put on gridiron, broil it; put butter, pepper, and salt on when broiling. After it is done, take 1 quart of oysters to one dish of fillets; drain the oysters of all liquor; fricassee them. Take 1 teacupful of cream, 1 tablespoonful of flour, 1 tablespoonful of butter, put in a little mace to season, and make a sauce; then put in the oysters, and let it boil up once to get done. Pour in 1 wine-glass of wine. Take your fish, lap the ends over each other on the dish; pour your oysters in center. Take 1 scoop French potatoes, and put four piles around the dish. These potatoes must be boiled in lard and seasoned to taste.

No. 54.

SADDLE OF VENISON.

[12 pounds.]

Take the top skin off. Take portion of fat out, skewer it pretty round; let it cook ¾ of an hour; cut it down in the back, take out the fillets, slice them, pepper and salt them, and put them back. Make a sauce of 1 cup of sugar, ½ cup of vinegar, 2 teacups of tomatoes, the essence out of the venison, 1 teaspoonful of nutmeg, ½ teacup of wine. Serve it with the venison. Make potato croquettes to put around the dish.

No. 55.

MUSHROOM CATSUP.

Full grown mushrooms are preferred. Put a layer of these in a deep earthen pan, and sprinkle them with salt; then another layer of mushrooms and more salt, and so on alternately salt and mushrooms. Let them remain 2 or 3 hours, by which time the salt will have gone all through the mushrooms, and make them easy to break; then pound them in a mortar or mash them well with your hands, and let them remain for a couple of days, not longer, stirring them up and mashing them well each day; then pour them in a stone jar, and to each quart add 1½ ounces of whole black pepper, ½ ounce of allspice; stop the jar very close, and set it in a stewpan of boiling water; let it boil for 2 hours. Take out the jar, and clear the juice of settlings by pouring through a hair sieve into a clean stewpan; let it boil gently for ½ hour. Keep in a dry, cool place; cork tightly or it will spoil.

No. 56.

WALNUT CATSUP.

Take 6 half sieves of green walnut shells, put them in a tub, mix well with common salt (from 2 to 3 pounds), let it stand for 6 days, frequently beating and mashing them; after a while the shells will become soft and pulpy. Pushing the shells up one side of the tub and tipping the tub a little, the liquor will run to the other side. This will be nice and clear. Take it out; repeat the above process until no more liquor can be obtained. You will get in all about 6 quarts. Let this simmer in an iron boiler as long as any scum rises. Bruise ¼ pound of ginger, ¼ pound of allspice, 2 ounces of long pepper, 2 ounces of cloves, put these in the liquor and boil slowly for ½ hour. When bottled put an equal quantity of spice in each bottle. When corked let the bottle be well filled up. Cork tightly, seal them over and put in a cool and dry place for 1 year.

No. 57.

MUSTARD QUICKLY MADE.

Mix very gradually and rub together in a mortar 1 ounce flour of mustard, 3 tablespoonfuls of milk or cream, ½ teaspoonful of salt, and same of sugar; rub together until smooth.

No. 57.

STUFFING FOR VEAL, TURKEY OR DUCK.

One-quarter pound of beef suet, ¼ pound of bread crumbs, 1 bunch of parsley, 1½ bunches of sweet marjoram or lemon thyme, a little grated lemon and onion chopped as fine as possible, a little pepper and salt; pound together with the yolk and white of 2 eggs, and secure it in the veal with a skewer, or sew it with a needle and thread.

No. 58.

OYSTER CATSUP.

Take fine, fresh oysters, wash them in their own liquor; skim it; pound them in a marble mortar; to 1 pint of oysters add 1 pint of sherry wine; boil them up; add 1 ounce of salt, 2 tablespoonfuls of pounded mace, and 1 tablespoonful of cayenne pepper; let it boil up again, skim it and rub it through a sieve, and when cold bottle it, cork it well and seal it up.

No. 59.

STUFFED PEPPERS.

One dozen green peppers; take out all the seed after cutting a piece off the top; lay them into cold water for 1½ hours; 1 pair sweetbreads, parboiled and skinned; 1 can mushrooms, 1 stalk of celery, 1 clove of garlic; chop up all fine; ½ loaf bread without crust. Grate up fine pepper and salt, a little nutmeg, ½ pound butter. Mix all up well; stuff the peppers with it. Put a piece of fat pork in your dripping pan; set the peppers up in the fat. Before putting in the oven put a little butter, melted, over them and sprinkle them with flour. When they commence to bake pour a little water in the pan and baste them well. Let it bake ½ hour in a steady oven. Cucumbers can be stuffed in the same way.

No. 60.

STUFFED QUAILS.

Take ½ or 1 dozen quails. Take the bone out same as in boned turkey. Put in mushrooms, truffles, bread crumbs. Make this stuffing moist with butter and pepper and salt. Be sure to stuff them tightly; tie them up, but do not take the feet off. Take a piece of larding pork and tie it on each bird's breast so as to keep it in shape. Then bake them in a baking pan, flour them and baste them. When done make a little sauce of currant jelly, 1 glass of wine, and the gravy from the birds. Lay the birds on a piece of buttered toast. Garnish the dish with cresses.

No. 61.

MUTTON-CHOPS.

Take 1 dozen mutton chops. Take the bone out of the chop; shape it as it was before the bone was taken out. Pepper and salt them; place them in beaten egg and then in bread crumbs. Put them in a skillet of hot lard; fry a delicate brown. Half peck of spinach, picked and clean, must be put into boiling water. Let it boil ten minutes. Place in cold water in a pan; after getting cool squeeze perfectly dry. Chop very fine; mix a tablespoonful of flour in it, 1 tablespoonful butter, gravy of any kind, or colored water of burnt sugar. Place in a stewpan with pepper and salt and a little nutmeg. Cover closely for 10 minutes to cook, and then for 5 minutes more with cover off. Be careful not to let it burn. Put the spinach in the centre of dish and set the chops up all around it. Boil 3 eggs; cut them in quarters and put around the dish.

No. 62.

CHEESE SOUFFLEE.

Take 3 tablespoonfuls flour, 1 of butter, a little chicken water or clear boiling water; cream the flour and butter together, pour chicken soup or boiling water over this till about the consistency of paste; take off the fire, let get cold, then put in fine-grated cheese (or English cheese), at the same time put in 5 yolks of eggs beaten up well in the batter, a little cayenne pepper and a little salt; beat the whites into a stiff froth; set them into a cool place, also the batter, but separately. When you send the dinner in beat the whites in with the batter and cook in moulds or paper cups or pudding-dish; let cook as speedily as possible and send directly to the table; must be served hot.

No. 63.

PLUM-PUDDING SAUCE.

Take a glass of sherry, ½ glass of brandy or essence of punch, 2 teaspoonfuls of pounded lump sugar, a little grated lemon peel; put all these in a ¼ pint of thick melted butter, grating nutmeg on top.

No. 64.

CAPER SAUCE.

One tablespoonful of capers and 2 tablespoonfuls of vinegar. To prepare the capers mince ⅓ of them very fine, divide the rest in halves; put them in a ¼ pint of melted butter or thickened gravy; stir them the same way as the melted butter or it will oil. A few leaves of parsley minced fine can be added to the sauce; keep the caper bottle corked closely; do not use any of the liquor; if the capers are not well covered with it they will spoil. This sauce is used with a boiled leg of mutton.

No. 65.

LOBSTER SAUCE.

Choose a fine hen lobster; let it be fresh; boil it; pick out the spawn and red coral in a mortar; add ½ ounce of butter, pound smooth, rub through a hair sieve with back of wooden spoon, cut lobster meat in small squares, put pounded spawn into as much melted butter as will do, and stir it together till mixed; now put in lobster meat and warm it on the fire; do not let it boil, as that will deprive it of its red color. Some use veal or beef gravy instead of melted butter.

No. 66.

MUSHROOM SAUCE.

Pick and peel ½ pint of mushrooms; wash clean and put in saucepan with ½ pint veal gravy or milk, a little pepper and salt, 1 ounce of butter rubbed with a tablespoonful of flour; stir them together and set them over a gentle fire and stew slowly till tender; skim and strain it.

No. 67.

MUSHROOM SAUCE—BROWN.

Put the mushrooms into ½ pint beef gravy, thicken with flour and butter and proceed as above.

No. 68.

TOMATO SAUCE.

Place on the fire the tomatoes, washed broth, onion, parsley, and seasonings; boil to a pulp about 35 minutes; rub through a fine sieve; return to the fire, make it hot, stir in the butter and serve.

No. 69.

CHROMSKIES.

Two cupfuls chicken, ½ cupful mushrooms, ½ cupful ham, yolks of 2 eggs, 1 small onion, 2 tablespoonfuls of chopped parsley, 1 level teaspoonful each of royal powder, celery, salt, and thyme, large pinch of salt, 1½ tablespoonfuls of butter, and 2 of flour, 1 cupful of broth. Cut the onion fine, fry it in the stewpan with the butter; when of a deep yellow add the flour, stir 2 minutes; add the broth boiling, the seasonings, and yolks; stir 4 minutes longer; add the fowl, ham, and mushrooms cut in small neat dice; set away to get firm by cooling; cut in neat pieces, dip in common butter, and fry in plenty of hot lard 5 minutes.

No. 70.

CABINET PUDDING A LA FRANCAISE.

Take ½ pound of lady-fingers and scrape the crust off; then butter them; take a fluted pudding mould, buttering it well, stick the lady-fingers up all around it. One-fourth pound candied cherries, ¼ pound citron, ¼ pound raisins, with seeds picked out, ¼ pound currants washed clean, ½ dozen macaroni. Take the scrapings and balance of lady-fingers, leaving out 8 for the top, and put all the fruit into these dry crumbs. Put all in the mould, with a layer of butter. Just before you put it on to boil take 5 whites and 7 yolks of 7 eggs, 1 quart of milk, make a custard, sweetened to taste. Pour it over the cake and fruit in the mould. Boil slowly 2½ hours. Take a tumbler of Jamaica rum, 1 tumbler milk, 2 eggs, and make a sauce. Stir till it almost comes to a boil and serve hot. Take the 2 whites of eggs, left of the 7 eggs used previously, and beat them very light, and put on top of pudding when taken out of mould. Drop a few candied cherries on top. Serve hot.

No. 71.

FISH PUDDING.

Three pounds of rock, boil it not quite done enough to serve; take it out; let it get cool; then take all the skin off; take the fish from the bones in fine pieces, not mashed up; ½ can of truffles; 1 can of mushrooms; peel the truffles; cut the largest size truffles and mushrooms into rose and star shapes with little cutters; take a 3-pint pudding mould fluted and grease it well, setting the shapes all around the mould; cut most of the mushrooms with a little parsley very fine and put with the fish; the truffles must be cut up and put in the sauce; ½ pint of milk, a full tablespoonful of flour, medium size tablespoonful of butter; mix the flour and butter together; put the milk on to boil; then pour it into the flour and butter; then pour all on the fish; put pepper and salt in it; put fish in a mould; cover it up tight and place it in a pot of boiling water two-thirds up the sides of the mould and let it steam ½ hour; take ½ pint of cream and mushroom water; put it on the fire to boil; rub up a tablespoonful each of flour and butter; mix all together, putting in the balance of the truffles and mushrooms, and let all boil 10 or 15 minutes; season with pepper and salt; 1 quart of scoop French potatoes; boil them done in salt and water; when done put through a colander. When it is time to serve the fish pudding pour the fish out into the platter and pour the potatoes around the dish; serve the gravy in a sauce-bowl.

No. 72.

SNIPE PUDDING.

Pick 8 fine, fat, fresh snipes; singe them; cut in halves; take out the gizzards and reserve the trail for further use; season the snipes with pepper, salt, lemon juice, and set aside till wanted; peel half of an onion; cut in thin slices, and fry in a stewpan with a little butter; when browned throw in a tablespoonful of flour; stir together on the fire for 3 minutes; add a handful of chopped mushrooms and parsley, a small bay-leaf, a sprig of thyme, a little mace, and a small silver onion; put in 1 pint of claret; stir the whole upon the fire, and when boiled 10 minutes add the trail and a small piece of breakfast bacon; let the sauce boil 3 minutes longer, and rub through the sieve upon the snipes; line a pudding-basin with suet-paste; fill it up with what has been prepared, and when covered with paste well fastened around the edge let it steam in a covered stewpan for 2½ hours; when done turn out of basin with care; pour a rich brown game gravy under it and serve.

No. 73.

BEEFSTEAK PUDDING.

Paste, 2½ pounds round steak, 1 level teaspoonful each of celery salt, thyme, and marjoram, 1 small onion, salt and white pepper to taste, 4 sprigs parsley. Line a well-buttered pudding mould with the paste, wet the edges, make a layer of beef, cut in neat scallops, sprinkle with the onion and parsley minced fine and mixed on a plate with celery salt, thyme, marjoram, salt and pepper, then another layer of beef, and seasoning, and so on until each is used; fill up with cold water, cover it with paste, place a buttered paper over it and set in a saucepan with boiling water to reach two-thirds up the outside of the mould; steam it thus 2½ hours, turn carefully out on a dish, pour over it any gravy that may be at hand, made hot and flavored with any kind of sauce piquante.

No. 74.

BOSTON BAKED PLUM PUDDING.

One-and-one-half cupfuls beef suet freed of skin and chopped very fine, 1½ cupfuls raisins stoned, 1½ cupfuls currants washed and picked, 1 cupful brown sugar, 2 cupfuls flour, 1 teaspoonful baking powder, 4 eggs, 1 cupful milk, ½ cupful citron chopped, pinch of salt, 1 tablespoonful extract of nutmeg, 1 glass of brandy. Put all these ingredients in a bowl, the eggs as they drop from the shell, the flour sifted with the powder and the brandy; mix into a rather short batter; pour into a well-buttered clean cake tin and bake in a steady oven two hours. Serve with vanilla sauce.

No. 75.

VANILLA SAUCE.

Put ½ pint milk in a small saucepan over the fire; when scalding hot add the yolks of 3 eggs, stir until it is as thick as boiled custard; add, when taken from the fire and cooled, 1 tablespoonful extract vanilla and whites of two eggs whipped stiff.

CABINET PUDDING, 2.

Four English muffins or rolls, ½ pint milk, 1 pint cream, 4 eggs and 4 yolks, 1 cupful sugar; ½ cupful almonds blanched, by pouring boiling water on them until the skins slip off easily, and cut into shreds; 1 cupful each dried cherries, apricots, green gages, or any other preserved, whole, or panned fruits; 1 glass noyeau. Well butter a mould; make a layer of muffins cut very thin, then of fruit, the almonds, and so on, until all the ingredients are used; beat the milk, cream, sugar, eggs, and noyeau together; pour over the contents of mould, and let it stay, before baking, at least half an hour; then set it in a saucepan with boiling water to reach two-thirds up the mould; steam it thus one hour; turn it out on a dish carefully and serve with cream sauce.

No. 77.

CREAM SAUCE.

Bring ⅔ pint of cream slowly to boil; set in stewpan of boiling water; when it reaches the boiling point, add the sugar; then pour it slowly on the whipped whites of eggs in a bowl; add 1 teaspoonful Royal extract vanilla, and use.

No. 78.

GREEN-CORN PUDDING.

Eight ears corn, 1 large teaspoonful butter, ½ cupful sugar, pinch of salt, 2 eggs, 1 pint of milk, 1 teaspoonful Royal extract of vanilla. Split each row on the cob lengthways; cut off the rounded point, and with the handle of the spoon push out the eyes and cream into a bowl; add to the milk, hot, the eggs, well beaten, the sugar, butter, and extract; pour it into a buttered dish, and bake 40 minutes in a moderate oven.

No. 79.

PLUM PUDDING.

Two cupfuls raisins, 2 cupfuls currants, 2 cupfuls suet, ½ cupful almonds blanched, 2 cupfuls flour, 2 cupfuls grated Royal sugar muffins or bread; ½ cupful each of citron, orange and lemon peel; 8 eggs, 1 cupful sugar, ½ cupful cream, 1 gill each of wine and brandy, large pinch salt, 1 tablespoonful Royal extract of nutmeg, 1 teaspoonful Royal baking-powder. Put in a large bowl the raisins seeded, the currants washed and picked, the suet chopped very fine, the almonds cut fine, the citron, orange and lemon peels chopped, the lemon, sugar, wine, brandy, and cream; lastly, add the flour, sifted, with the powder, and mix all well together; put in a large, well-buttered mould, set in a saucepan with boiling water to reach one-half up the sides of the mould, and steam it thus five hours; turn out on its dish carefully and serve with hot brandy sauce.

No. 80.

TAPIOCA PUDDING.

One cupful tapioca, soaked in 1 quart cold water over night, 1 cupful sugar, 1½ pints milk, and 4 eggs.

No. 81.

CABINET PUDDING, 1.

Half pound of stale sponge cake, ½ cup of raisins, ½ can of peaches, 4 eggs, and 1½ pints of milk. Butter a plain oval mould; lay in some of the stale cake, ⅓ of the raisins, stoned, ⅓ of the peaches; make two layers of the remainder of the cake, raisins, and peaches; cover with a very thin slice of bread, then pour over the milk, beaten with eggs and sugar; set in a sauce pan with boiling water, to reach two-thirds up the side of the mould; steam it ¾ of an hour, and turn out carefully on a dish. Serve with peach sauce.

No. 82.

CUSTARD PUDDING.

One and a half pints of milk, 4 eggs, 1 cupful of sugar, 2 teaspoonfuls Royal extract of vanilla. Beat the eggs and sugar together; dilute with the milk and extract; pour into a buttered pudding dish, set in the oven in a dripping-pan two-thirds full of boiling water; bake until firm, about 40 minutes, in a moderate oven.

No. 83.

PLUM PUDDING.

Two cupfuls each of stoned raisins and currants, washed and picked, beef-suet chopped fine, and coffee sugar, 3 cupfuls of grated English muffins or bread, 8 eggs 1 cupful each, chopped citron and almonds, blanched by pouring boiling water over them till the skins slip off easily, and 1 lemon peel, and a pinch of salt. Mix all these ingredients in a large bowl, put in a well-buttered mould, set in a saucepan with boiling water to reach two-thirds up its sides, steam it thus 5 hours; turn it out carefully on its dish, and serve with brandy poured over it, and brandy sauce in a bowl. When about to serve on the table, the brandy should be set on fire.

No. 84.

RICE PUDDING.

One cupful of rice, 1 quart of milk, 4 eggs, 1 tablespoonful of butter, 1 cupful of sugar, and a pinch of salt. Boil the rice in 1 pint of milk until tender, then remove it from the fire; add the eggs, sugar, salt, and milk, beaten together, and mix; pour into a pudding dish, break the butter in small pieces on the surface, and bake in a steady oven 30 minutes. Serve with brandy sauce.

No. 85.

CUSTARD SAUCE.

One pint of milk, yolks of 4 eggs, ½ cupful sugar. Set on the fire, and stir until thick.

No. 86.

ROYAL WINE SAUCE.

Bring slowly to the boiling point ½ pint of wine, then add to it the yolks of 4 eggs, and 1 cupful of sugar; whip it on the fire until it is in a state of high froth, and a little thick; remove and use as directed.

No. 87.

PRINCESS PUDDING.

Two-thirds of a cupful of butter, 1 cupful of sugar, 1 large cupful of flour, 3 eggs, ½ teaspoonful Royal baking powder, and a small glass of brandy. Rub to a smooth cream butter and sugar, add the eggs, one at a time, beating a few minutes between; add the flour, sifted, with the powder and the brandy; put into a mould, well buttered; set in saucepan with boiling water to reach half up its sides; steam it thus 1½ hours, turn on its dish carefully, and serve with lemon sauce.

No. 88.

YORKSHIRE PUDDING.

Three-quarters of pint of flour, 3 eggs, 1½ pints of milk, a pinch of salt, 1½ teaspoonfuls of Royal baking powder. Sift the flour and powder together, add eggs, beaten, with the milk; stir quickly into a rather thinner batter than for griddle cakes; pour it into a dripping pan, plentifully spread with cold beef drippings; bake in oven 25 minutes. Serve with roast beef.

No. 89.

COTTAGE PUDDING.

Make a sponge cake—about a ½-pound mould sponge cake; ¼ pound almonds, blanch them. When the cake is done stick these almonds all over it. Pour ½ pint sherry wine all over it. Cover it up and set it away till time to serve. Take 1 quart of milk, boil it, 7 yolks of eggs; mix with sugar to taste essence of lemon or vanilla. When the milk boils pour it on the eggs. Pour it in a saucepan and just let it come almost to a boil, so as to thicken it. Take it off the fire and set in an ice-box to let it get cold. Beat the whites of eggs to a stiff froth; put in it while beating a little apple, raspberry, or currant jelly, or any kind of preserve. When ready to serve pour the custard on the cake and put the icing all over the custard.

No. 90.

VERMICELLI PUDDING.

Boil 1 pint of milk with lemon peel and cinnamon, sweeten with loaf sugar, strain through a sieve, adding ¼ pound of vermicelli; boil 10 minutes, put in the yolks of 5 eggs and the whites of 3 eggs. Mix well together and steam 1¼ hours. Bake ½ hour.

No. 91.

BOILED CUSTARDS.

Put 1 quart of new milk in a stewpan, with the peel of a lemon cut very thin, a little grated nutmeg, a bay or laurel leaf, small stick of cinnamon. Set over a quick fire. Don't let it boil over. When boiled set off on one side of stove. Let simmer 10 minutes. Break the yolks of 8 eggs and the whites of 4 eggs in a basin; beat them well; then pour in the milk, a little at a time, stirring as quickly as possible so the eggs will not curdle. Set on the fire again, stirring it. Let boil up once; pass it through a fine sieve. When cold add brandy or white wine. Serve up in glasses or cups. Custards for baking have a little nutmeg grated over them. Bake 15 or 20 minutes.

No. 92.

ROMAN PUNCH.

Make 2 quarts of lemonade, rich with the pure juice of lemon and add to this 1 tablespoonful of the extract of lemon; work this well and freeze; just before serving up and for each quart of the ice ½ pint of cognac and ½ pint Jamaica rum. Mix well and serve in high glasses, as this makes what is called a semi or half ice. It is usually served at dinners as a coup d'milieu.

No. 93.

TRANSPARENT ICING.

Place 1 pound pulverized white sugar in a basin with ½ pint water. Boil to the consistency of mucilage, then rub the sugar with a wooden spatula against the sides of the pans until it assumes a milky appearance. Stir in 2 tablespoonfuls extract vanilla; mix well together. Pour this while hot over the top of cake so as to completely cover it.

No. 94.

COFFEE ICE CREAM.

One quart best cream, ½ pint of strong Mocha coffee, 14 ounces white pulverized sugar, 8 yolks eggs. Mix these ingredients in a porcelain-lined basin; place on fire to thicken; rub through a hair sieve into a basin; put into freezer and freeze.

No. 95.

ITALIEN ORANGE ICE CREAM.

One and one-half pints best cream, 12 ounces white pulverized sugar, the juice of 6 oranges, and 2 teaspoonfuls orange extract, the yolks of 8 eggs, and a pinch of salt. Mix these ingredients in a porcelain-lined basin, and stir over fire until the composition begins to thicken; rub and pass the cream through a hair sieve; put into freezer and finish.

No. 96.

RASPBERRY WATER ICE.

Press sufficient raspberries through a hair sieve to give 3 pints of juice. Add 1 pound pulverized white sugar and the juice of 1 lemon. Place in freezer and freeze.

No. 97.

CHOCOLATE ICE CREAM.

Three pints best cream, 12 ounces pulverized white sugar, 4 whole eggs, a tablespoonful extract vanilla, a pint rich cream whipped, 6 ounces chocolate; dissolve in a small quantity of milk to a smooth paste; now mix it with the cream, sugar, eggs and extract. Place all on the fire and stir until it begins to thicken; strain through a hair sieve, place in freezer, and when nearly frozen stir in lightly the whipped cream.

No. 98.

LEMON WATER ICE.

Juice of 6 lemons, 2 teaspoonfuls extract lemon, 1 quart water, 1 pound granulated sugar, 1 gill rich sweet cream; add all together and strain. Freeze same as ice cream.

No. 99.

ORANGE WATER ICE.

Juice of 6 oranges, 2 teaspoonfuls extract orange, juice of 1 lemon, 1 quart water, 1 pound granulated sugar, 1 gill rich sweet cream; add all together and strain. Freeze same as ice cream.

No. 100.

SULTANA CAKE.

Two cupfuls butter, 1½ cupfuls sugar, 6 eggs, ½ cupful thick cream, 1½ pints flour, 1 teaspoonful of baking powder, 4 cupfuls sultana raisins, ½ cupful of chopped citron. Rub the butter and sugar to a very light cream; add the eggs, 2 at a time, beating 5 minutes between each addition; add the flour, sifted with the powder, the cream, raisins, and citron. Mix into a rather firm batter, put into a paper-lined cake-tin, and bake in a moderate oven 1¼ hours. When removed from the oven carefully spread a little transparent icing.

No. 101.

VARIEGATED CAKES.

One cup powdered sugar, ½ cup of butter creamed with the sugar, ½ cup of milk, 4 eggs, the whites whipped only, whipped light; 2½ cups of prepared flour, bitter almond flavoring, spinach juice, and cochineal, cream, butter and sugar; add the milk, flavoring, whites and flour. Divide the latter into three parts. Bruise and pound a few leaves of spinach in thin muslin bags until you can express the juice. Put a few drops of this into one portion of the batter; color another with cochineal, leaving the third white. Put a little of each into small round pans or cups, giving a little stir to each color as you add the next. This will vein the cakes prettily. Put the white between the pink and green that the tints may show better. If you can get pistachionuts to pound up for the green the cakes will be much nicer. Ice on sides and top.

No. 102.

SWISS PANCAKES.

One-half cupful butter, ½ cupful sugar, 1½ cupfuls flour, 1 teaspoonful baking powder, 1 large apple peeled, cored, and minced fine, ½ pint milk, ½ pint cream, 1 teaspoonful each extract of nutmeg and cinnamon, 4 eggs. Sift the flour with the powder, add to it the butter, melted, the sugar and eggs beaten together and diluted with the milk, cream, and extracts. Have a piece of butter melted in a small round frying-pan, pour in it about ½ cupful of butter; turn the frying-pan round that the batter may cover it; fry on one side only. Serve them piled one on the other, with sugar strewed between the cakes.

No. 103.

GERMAN PANCAKES.

Proceed as directed for Swiss pancakes, spreading pastry cream between each, and serve with currant jelly sauce.

No. 104.

SCOTCH PANCAKES.

One pint of milk, 2 tablespoonfuls butter, 4 eggs, 2/3 cupful of flour, 1 tablespoonful baking-powder; a pinch of salt; sift the flour, salt, and powder together, add the milk, eggs, and butter melted; mix into a thin batter; have a small round frying-pan, with a little butter melted in it; pour in ½ cupful of batter; turn the pan round to cover it with the batter; place on a sharp fire to brown; then hold it up in front of the fire, and the pancake will rise up; spread each with marmalade or jelly, roll it up and serve with sliced lemon and sugar.

No. 105.

FRENCH PANCAKES.

Six tablespoonfuls of flour, 1 quart of milk, 5 eggs, 1 teaspoonful baking-powder, 1 tablespoonful of butter, two tablespoonfuls of sugar, nutmeg to taste; mix the flour, eggs, butter, sugar and 1 pint of milk together so as to make a thick batter; pour in the other pint of milk, add the powder and serve with either wine or cream sauce.

No. 106.

PUMPKIN PIE.

Paste, 1 pint of stewed pumpkin, 3 eggs, 1½ pints of milk, 2 teaspoonfuls of ginger, 1 teaspoonful each nutmeg, cloves, cinnamon, and mace, a pinch of salt and 1 cupful of sugar. Stew the pumpkin as follows: Cut a pumpkin of a deep color, firm and close in texture, in half; remove the seeds, but do not peel it; cut in small slices, and put in a shallow stewpan with about ½ cupful of water; cover very light, and as soon as steam forms set it where it will not burn; when the pumpkin is tender turn off the liquor and set it back on the stove to steam-dry; then measure out, after straining, one pint; add the milk boiling, the sugar mixed with the spices and salt, and mix well together; add the eggs beaten last; line a pie-plate, well greased, with the paste; make a thick rim round the edge, pour in the prepared pumpkin, and bake in quick, steady oven about 30 minutes till the pie is firm in the center.

No. 107.

GINGER CAKE.

Three-fourths of a cupful of butter, 2 cupfuls of sugar, 4 eggs, 1½ teaspoonfuls of baking-powder, 1½ pints of flour, 1 cupful of milk, 1 tablespoonful of extract of ginger; rub the butter and sugar to a light cream, add the eggs 2 at a time, beating 5 minutes between; add the flour sifted with the powder, the milk and extract; mix into a smooth, medium batter; bake in a cake tin in a rather hot oven 40 minutes.

No. 108.

HUCKLEBERRY CAKE.

One cupful of butter, 2 cupfuls of brown sugar, 4 eggs, 1½ pints of flour, 2 teaspoonfuls of baking powder, 2 cupfuls of huckleberries washed and picked, 1 teaspoonful each of extract cloves, cinnamon, and allspice, one cupful of milk; rub the butter and sugar to a light cream; add the eggs 2 at a time, beating 5 minutes between; add flour sifted with the powder, huckleberries, extracts and mix; mix in a batter; put into a paper-lined cake tin, bake in a quick oven 50 minutes.

No. 109.

JUMBLES.

One and one-half cupfuls of butter, 2 cupfuls of sugar, 6 eggs, 1½ pints of flour, ½ cupful of cornstarch, 1 teaspoonful of baking powder, 1 teaspoonful of extract of lemon, ½ cupful of chopped peanuts mixed with ½ cupful of granulated sugar; beat the butter and sugar smooth; add the beaten eggs, the flour, the cornstarch, and powder sifted together, and the extract; flour the board; roll out the dough rather thin; cut out with biscuit cutter; roll in the chopped peanuts and sugar; lay on greased baking tin; bake in rather hot oven 8 to 10 minutes.

No. 110.

WHITE SPONGE CAKE.

Whites of 8 eggs, 1 cupful of sugar, ½ cupful of flour, ½ of cornstarch, 1 teaspoonful of baking powder, 1 teaspoonful of extract of rose; sift the flour, cornstarch, sugar, and powder together; add it to the whites of the eggs whipped to a dry froth, and the extract, mix gently but thoroughly; bake in a cake-mould well buttered, in a quick oven 30 minutes.

No. 111.

MADELAINES.

One cupful of butter, 1 cupful of sugar, 3 eggs, 1½ cupfuls of flour, ½ teaspoonful of baking powder, 1 glass of brandy, 1 teaspoonful of the extract of cinnamon, slightly melt the butter in a cake bowl; add the sugar and eggs; stir a few minutes; add the flour, sifted, with the powder, the extract, and the brandy; mix into a batter that will almost run; bake in well-greased muffin-pans in a moderate oven 20 minutes; pour on the top of each a little transparent icing to cover, and add a few colored comfits.

No. 112.

QUEEN CAKE.

Two cupfuls of butter, 2½ cupfuls of sugar, 1½ pints of flour, 8 eggs, ½ teaspoonful baking powder, 1 wineglass each of wine, brandy, and cream, ½ teaspoonful of the extract of nutmeg, rose, and lemon, 1 cupful of dried currants washed and picked, 1 cupful of raisins, stoned and cut in two; 1 cupful of citron cut in small, thin slices; rub the butter and sugar to a very light cream; add the eggs, 2 at a time, beating 5 minutes between each addition; add the flour, sifted, with the powder, the raisins, currants, wine, brandy, cream, citron, and extracts; mix into a consistent batter, and bake carefully in a papered cake-tin in a moderate, steady oven 1½ hours.

No. 113.

CREAM CAKES.

Ten eggs, ½ cupful of butter, ¾ pound of flour, 1 pint of water, 1½ pints of milk, 3 large tablespoonfuls of cornstarch, 2 cupfuls of sugar, yolks of 5 eggs, 1 large tablespoonful of good butter, and 2 teaspoonfuls of the extract of vanilla; set the water on the fire in a stewpan with the butter; as soon as it boils stir in the sifted flour with a wooden spoon; stir vigorously until it leaves the bottom and sides of the pan when removed from the fire, and beat in the eggs one at a time; place this batter into a pointed canvas bag having a nozzle at the small end; press out the batter in the shape of fingers on a greased baking tin a little distance apart; bake in a steady brick oven 20 minutes; when cold cut the sides and fill with pastry cream.

No. 114.

PASTRY CREAM.

Bring the milk to a boil with the sugar; add the starch dissolved in a little water; as soon as it reboils take from the fire; beat in the egg yolks; return to the fire 2 minutes to set the eggs; add the extract and butter; when cold use it.

No. 115.

CHOCOLATE CREAM.

Set on the fire 1 gill of water, 1½ cupfuls sugar, ½ cup of grated chocolate, in a small saucepan; boil till it gets thick and looks velvety; then take off the fire, and add the whites of 2 eggs, without beating: use it hot, covering the top and sides of the cake. As it cools it grows firm.

No. 116.

SPONGE CAKE, No. 2.

Six eggs, 3 cupfuls sugar, 4 cupfuls flour, 2 teaspoonfuls baking-powder, 1 cupful cold water, pinch of salt, 1 teaspoonful extract of lemon. Beat the eggs and sugar together 5 minutes; add the flour, sifted, with the salt and powder, the water and extract; bake in a shallow square cake-pan, in a quick, steady oven, 35 minutes; when removed from the oven, ice it with clear icing, made of 1 cupful sugar, 1 tablespoonful lemon juice, and whites of 2 eggs; mix together, smooth, and pour over cake. If the cake is not hot enough to dry it, place it in the mouth of a moderately warm oven.

No. 117.

SPICE CAKE.

One cupful butter, 2 cupfuls sugar, 3 cupfuls flour, 1 teaspoonful baking-powder, 2 eggs, 1 cupful milk, ½ cupful each of raisins stoned, currants washed and picked; 1 teaspoonful each of extract of nutmeg, cloves, and cinnamon. Rub the butter and sugar to a light white cream; add the eggs, 1 at a time, beating a few minutes between each; add the flour, sifted, with the powder, the milk, fruit, and extracts; mix into a smooth, rather firm, batter; put into a paper-lined cake-tin and bake in a steady oven 30 minutes.

No. 118.

SCOTCH CAKE.

One and a half cupfuls butter, 2½ cupfuls sugar, 8 eggs, 1½ pints flour, ½ teaspoonful baking-powder, 3 cupfuls raisins, stoned, 1 tablespoonful extract of lemon. Rub the butter and sugar to a light white cream; add the eggs, 2 at a time, beating 5 minutes between each addition; add the flour, sifted, with the powder, the raisins and extract; mix into a smooth, consistent batter; put in a paper-lined square shallow cake-pan, and bake in a moderate oven 1 hour.

No. 119.

SHREWSBURY CAKE.

One cupful of butter, 3 cupfuls of sugar, 1½ pints of flour, 3 eggs, 1 teaspoonful of baking powder, 1 cupful of milk. Rub the butter and sugar to a smooth, white cream, add the eggs, 1 at a time, beating 5 minutes between each; add the flour, sifted, with the powder and the extract; mix into a medium batter, bake in a cake mould well and carefully greased, in a quick oven over 40 minutes.

No. 120.

VANILLA CAKE.

One and one half cupfuls of butter, 2 cupfuls of sugar, 6 yolks of eggs, 1 pint of flour, 1½ teaspoonfuls of baking powder, 1 cupful of cream, 1 tablespoonful of extract of vanilla. Rub the butter and sugar to a very light cream; add the egg yolks and cream, flour, sifted, with the powder and the extract; mix into a firm but smooth batter; bake in a shallow, square pan in a fairly hot oven, 35 minutes.

No. 121.

WINE CAKE.

One and one-half cupfuls of butter, 2 cupfuls of sugar, 2 cupfuls of flour, ½ teaspoonful of baking powder, 1 gill of wine, 3 eggs. Rub the butter and sugar to a light cream; add the eggs, 1 at a time, beating 5 minutes between each; add the flour, sifted, with the powder and the wine; mix into a medium firm batter; bake in a shallow, square cake pan in moderate oven 40 minutes; when taken from the oven carefully ice with the transparent icing.

No. 122.

DELICATE CAKE.

One and one-half cupfuls of butter, 1½ cupfuls of sugar, whites of five eggs, 2½ pints of flour, 1½ teaspoonfuls of baking powder, 1 cupful of milk, 1 teaspoonful of extract of peach. Rub the butter and sugar to a light cream; add the egg whites, 1 at a time, beating a few minutes between each; add the flour, sifted, with the powder, then the extract and milk; mix into a rather thin batter; pour into a paper-lined tin, and bake in a rather hot but steady oven 50 minutes.

No. 123.

DUCHESSE CAKE.

One and one-half cupful butter, 1 cupful sugar, 6 eggs, 1 teaspoonful baking powder, 1 pint flour, 1 teaspoonful extract cinnamon. Rub the butter and sugar to a light cream, add the eggs, 2 at a time, beating 10 minutes between each addition. Sift together flour and powder, add to the butter, etc., with the extracts; mix into a medium thick batter, and bake in small shallow square pans, lined with thin white paper, in a steady oven 30 minutes. When they are taken from the oven ice them.

MINCE PIES.

Mince-meat—Two pounds meat, 1 pound raisins, 1 pound currants, ½ pound citron, 1 pound chopped apples, 1 pound suet. Chop all up fine, except ½ each of currants and raisins. Put in 1 stick of preserved ginger or cherries, ½ pint brandy, ½ pint wine, nutmeg, ground allspice, ground cinnamon, mace to taste, sugar, and ½ pint cider. Make pie-crust or puff-paste.

No. 125.

CHARLOTTE RUSSE.

One quart charlotte mould, ¼ pound lady-fingers; line the mould with them; let the mould be dry. One quart cream sweetened to taste, flavored with pineapple, lemon, or other flavor, ¼ box gelatine dissolved in a little of the cream, cream whipped to a light, stiff froth. Set an extra pan on the ice and put all the whipped cream in it, then stir in gelatine. Put it in the mould, cover the top with lady-fingers, and set on ice to cool.

No. 126.

WAFFLES.

One pint flour, ½ yeast cake; make a batter over night with warm milk and set it to rise. In the morning beat light 3 eggs, 1 tablespoonful sugar, nutmeg to taste, 1 tablespoonful melted butter. Stir and put to rise till time to bake. Bake in moulds and sift a little powdered sugar over them and send to table.

No. 127.

BISCUITS.

One quart flour, 1 tablespoonful yeast powder, 1 tablespoonful butter or lard. Mix all together with milk; add 1½ teaspoonfuls of salt. Make your biscuits quick and bake in a hot oven.

No. 128.

CORN BREAD.

One pint meal, ½ pint hot water, ½ pint milk, mixed; 1 tablespoonful butter, yolks of 3 eggs, 1 teaspoonful yeast powder. Mix all together to a stiff batter. When ready to bake beat to a stiff froth the whites of the eggs, put it in, and put in baking mould in a hot oven.

No. 129.

SPONGE BREAD.

Take 2 Irish potatoes, boil them, mash fine when done, put into them 2 tablespoonfuls of flour, pour in the water the potatoes were boiled in, pour in the yeast, and let it rise. Make your bread up over night, either light bread or rolls. Your oven must bake even and steady or your bread will not be light.

No. 130.

SWEET POTATO PIE.

Boil 1 large sweet potato for 2 pies; mash through a wire sieve, 3 eggs, the yolks of which must be beaten up with the potato, sugar to taste, a little grated lemon peel, little nutmeg and cinnamon; grate all up together; 1 teacupful of milk, 1 tablespoonful of melted butter; when ready to make the pies beat the white to a stiff froth and stir in. Make the paste as directed in vol-au-vents.

No. 131.

HOW TO MAKE GOOD BREAD.

Sift your flour into your mixing-pan, warming it a little in cold weather, and make a hole in the center, and into this hole pour your sponge and stir the whole to the consistency of cake, and then let it stand in a warm place until it rises and becomes very light; then knead it thoroughly from all sides, adding flour as needed, and when it will not stick to your fingers or the side of the pan, set it aside until it rises again; then make it into five or six loaves, put them into your baking pans, and set them away in a warm place until it raises nicely, and then put it into the oven and bake it. A little experimenting will soon make you an efficient baker.

No. 132.

LIGHT BREAD.

Three pints of flour, half yeast cake dissolved in warm water, tablespoonful each of salt, lard, and white sugar, 1½ pints of potato water (warm), work hard, and let rise over night. In the morning mould and let rise again half an hour before baking; if too stiff add a little warm water, as it is better if made up rather soft. It will rise sooner and keep fresh longer. Always sift your flour before using, warming a little in cold weather; sifting twice gets more air between the particles. Do not have the oven too hot.

HOW TO MAKE GOOD YEAST.

Take 6 large sound potatoes, 1 gallon of water, and 2 ordinary handfuls of hops; put the potatoes, after peeling them, into the water, tie the hops into a bag, and boil all together till the potatoes are soft enough to mash easily; throw the hops away, put a cupful of flour in a large dish, take the potatoes out of the water, mash them through a colander, and mix them well with the flour; then pour the water used in boiling the potatoes over them, and mix the whole thoroughly; let the mixture stand till about milkwarm, and then add about a cent's worth of baker's yeast or an yeast cake, or a cupful of dry yeast, and after stirring it again set the whole, away over night; in the morning add a half cup of sugar, a half cup of salt, and a small tablespoonful of ginger; put the whole in a two gallon jug, and use a cupful of this yeast at a baking for five or six ordinary-sized loaves. When you make your next lot of yeast use a cupful of this yeast instead of the baker's or other yeast called for above.

CALVES'-FEET JELLY.

Get 4 calves' feet at the butcher's, cut them in two, and take away the fat from between the claws, wash them well in luke-warm water; put them in a large stewpan, and cover them with water. When the liquor boils, skim well and let it boil gently 6 or 7 hours, so as to reduce the quantity to 2 quarts; then strain through a sieve and skim off all the oily substance. If not in a hurry it is better to boil the calves' feet the day before you make the jelly, as it will skim better when perfectly cold, and the liquor part becomes firm. Put the liquor in a stewpan to melt, with a lump of sugar, the peel of 2 lemons, the juice of 6, and 6 whites and shells of eggs; beat together, with a bottle of sherry or Madeira. Stir the whole together till on a boil, then set on side of stove, and let simmer ¼ hour, and strain through a jelly-bag. Then pour back in bag again and strain till it is as bright and clear as rock-water. Put jelly in moulds to get firm and cold. If made in warm weather ice is required.

CHICKEN GLACEE.

Bone a chicken, stuff it with truffles, mushrooms, slight, ¼ pound ham, ½ pound veal, a little sweet marjoram and thyme, and a very small onion. Take the meat and one-half of the mushrooms and chop them up fine, and the other half cut in slices, and also the truffles must be peeled and cut in slices. Let the truffles be in a quarter size can. Mix all this together, and season with pepper and salt, then stuff it in the chicken. Put it in a bag tied up tightly, and let it boil 2 hours. Now take the carcass and giblets and boil them to make stock of. Make about 3 pints. Skim all the grease off top, take it off the stove, and let it get cold. Take one package of gelatine and put it in soup; after melting it clarify it with the white of an egg. Season with pepper and salt and a little nutmeg. Let it boil ten minutes, strain through a flannel bag, and set aside to cool. Take the chicken, put a heavy press on it, and let it get cold. Take a jelly mould and line it with boiled egg, mushrooms, and truffles, cut into stars and flower shapes; then a layer of jelly, then a layer of sliced chicken, till the mould is full. Set away in ice-box to get cold. Garnish the dish when ready to use with water-cresses or parsley.

No. 136.

CLAM CHOWDER.

Three pints of clams; scald them and take the hearts out; 1 pint tomatoes, boil and strain them through sieve, putting a tablespoonful of sugar in them; tablespoonful fine chopped onion, and a teaspoonful thyme, a small stalk of celery, chopped fine, ¼ pound butter and 2 two tablespoonfuls of flour, mixed in a stewpan; this must be placed together with the liquor from the clams, thyme, celery, onions, tomatoes, and ½ pint of cream. Let all boil together; season with pepper and salt, mace, and nutmeg to taste. Just before dishing up put in the clams. Let it boil up once.

No. 137.

CURRANT JELLY.

One peck of currants, put into a kettle, mashed; let boil up ten minutes; strain a few at a time through a cloth till all the juice is out; 1 pint of juice to 1 pound of sugar; put in preserving kettle, notice the hour it comes to a boil; let it boil 20 minutes, skimming all the time; put into glasses and place out in the hot sun, uncovered, for three days, then cover over with pieces of paper wet with brandy. Set away in a dry place.

No. 138.

VINEGAR PEACHES.

One peck Heath peaches (cling-stones) peeled over night; sprinkle 1 pound of sugar over them; in the morning drain off, put in ½ pint of cider vinegar, let vinegar and juice boil together, putting in a few peaches at a time, letting them boil just enough so that you can stick a straw through the peaches (15 minutes), have your jars sitting in hot water on the stove; put in your peaches as they get done; when the jars are full pour the syrup over them, then fasten them up while on the stove; let stay 15 minutes.

No. 139.

TOMATO CHOW-CHOW.

Fifty cucumbers, 50 green tomatoes, 2 dozen white onions, cut them up in slices over night, sprinkle with salt; in the morning place them in a colander and drain them dry; 1 pint of vinegar, ½ pound of brown sugar, 1 teaspoonful of tamarack, 1 teaspoonful black pepper, 1 tablespoonful each of allspice and cloves, ½ dozen leaves of mace. Put all these in a pot and let them come to a boil; after boiling take them out and put them in a jar covered up tightly.

No. 140.

MANGOES.

Take a mango, cut it, take all the seeds out, put in salt and water for 5 days, let them stay 1 day and night in clear water, drain them and stuff them with the following: Chop a hard head of cabbage, horseradish, mustard seed, garlic, a few cloves; and stuff each one, then tie on the piece taken off to make an opening to take the seeds out. Boil sufficient vinegar to cover them, putting cloves and allspice in the vinegar; pour this over them in the jars; continue boiling the vinegar, pouring it off and on the mangoes for three days; then fasten up for use.

No. 141.

SWEET POTATO PIE.

Boil 2 good-sized sweet potatoes, weighing about a pound; strain and mash through a sieve; 1 tablespoonful of butter must be put in them; sweeten to taste; 1 pint of boiling milk, 5 yolks of eggs, must be well beaten into the potatoes; stir the hot milk in on them. Grate in a little lemon peel; nutmeg to taste; put in 1 teaspoonful essence of lemon; beat up the whites of eggs into the potatoes, make a puff paste, roll out and make pies without tops.

Custard pies can be made in the same way, leaving out the potatoes.

In lemon pies use same quantity of ingredients as above, using 3 lemons.

No. 142.

MERINGUE PIE.

One cup of sugar, yolks of 3 eggs, 1½ cups of milk, 2 teaspoonfuls of corn starch, juice and grated peel of 1 lemon. Beat the yolks light and add the sugar, rub the cornstarch in with milk, and add that, and then the lemon, and beat well together. Line some pans with a rich paste, and then fill with the custard, and bake. When done take the whites of 3 eggs and beat them with a tablespoonful of sugar to a stiff froth, which spread over the top, and brown in the oven.

No. 143.

SWEET POTATO PUDDING.

Half pound of butter, ½ pound of sugar, 5 eggs, 2 tablespoonfuls of brandy, same of rose-water; add 1 pound of sweet potatoes, boiled and mashed fine, with a pinch of salt and a little milk to make it moist. Beat the butter and eggs and sugar till light, to which add the potatoes, a small quantity at a time; whisk the eggs till thick, and stir in gradually; then add the brandy and rose-water. Mix all well together, and set aside in a cool place for awhile. This is enough for 3 or 4 puddings, soup-plate size. Line your plates with a nice paste, fill and bake in a quick oven. Nutmeg or cinnamon can be substituted for the rose-water if desired.

No. 144.

COCOANUT PUDDING.

Half pound of sugar, ½ pound of butter, ½ pound of grated cocoanut, the whites of 6 eggs, 1 tablespoonful of rose-water, 2 tablespoonfuls of brandy; beat the sugar and butter to a cream, whisk the whites of the eggs till they are stiff, which beat into the butter and sugar; stir the whole together and add gradually the nut, brandy, and rose-water; do not beat it. This will make two full-sized puddings. Line your plates with rich paste; fill and bake in a quick oven.

No. 145.

PUFF PUDDING.

Mix 2 cups of flour with ⅔ of a cup of butter, and 2 cups of sugar. Dissolve 3 teaspoonfuls of good baking powder in 1 cup of milk and 1 teaspoonful of essence of lemon and half a nutmeg. Take 4 eggs—keep the whites of 2 for frosting—and beat the others thoroughly; then mix all together, and bake in a quick oven. When done frost the top with the reserved whites, well beaten, with a small quantity of powdered sugar.

No. 146.

PUFF PASTE.

Take 1 pound of best quality of flour, sifted, 1 pound of good, firm, sweet butter or lard, or equal parts of each; divide the shortening into quarters; take one quarter and chop it fine, and mix it with the flour with a knife, as the warmth from the hands will make the butter soft; then with a small quantity of cold water make into a stiff dough; flour the board, turn out the paste, dredge with flour, and roll thin; then cut another quarter of the shortening into thin slices, and lay on the paste, dredge with flour, fold over the sides, forming a square; then roll again and add another quarter of the shortening, and so continue till all the shortening is rolled in. Handle as little as possible. When done, roll about half inch thick, cut into quarters, place on a plate, and set aside in a cool place for 2 hours. Take only as much as you want for one crust, dredge the board, and roll out, making it thinner at the middle than on the edges, which should be one quarter of an inch thick; grease the pans, lay on the paste, pressing it lightly into form, and trim the edge with a knife; put in the filling, cover with another paste as before, trim and ornament the edges, if desired, and bake in a quick oven.

No. 147.

FILLET OF CHICKENS.

Take the breasts of 4 chickens (tender). This is sufficient for twelve persons. Take 4 fillets out of each chicken; then cut them into a shape something like the breastbone of a chicken; take the skin off, flatten them with a mallet; butter a skillet; lay them close together in it; then pour ½ pint of milk and ½ pint of stock over them; put a weight over them and let them simmer till tender; after they are done, slice some mushrooms and truffles and put one of each, forming a row, on each breast; round them on a platter, then take the essence and put ½ pint of cream in it, making a rich sauce; ¾ of a pint of spinach; take all the stems off and parboil the leaves; take them out of the hot water and put them into cold water; then squeeze them dry out of this and chop very fine; 1 tablespoonful each of flour and butter and mix them up into the chopped spinach; 1 teacup of stock is poured over this and thoroughly mixed in it; pepper, salt, grated nutmeg; then put it on the fire, stewing slowly for 20 minutes; boil hard three eggs; cut in slices; put spinach in the center of the dish, chicken around it; pour sauce all round; put sliced egg around the spinach; serve hot.

No. 148.

JURY PIE.

Steam and boil some mealy potatoes; then mash them with some butter or cream; season to taste and place a layer at the bottom of a pie dish; upon this put a layer of fine-chopped cold meat or any kind of fish well seasoned; then another layer of potatoes and more chopped meat, alternately, till the dish is filled; smooth down the top; strew breadcrumbs upon it and bake till well browned. This will make a nice little dish. Chopped pickles may be added. Should you use fish instead of meat, first beat it up in raw egg. It will taste better. Dressed spinach, tomatoes, asparagus tops may be used in place of meat, but there should be more potatoes than anything else in the pie.

No. 149.

POTATO PIE.

Four large potatoes boiled and mashed with butter and cream; ½ pound of butcher's meat; ¼ pound of ham or bacon cut small or chopped; hard boiled eggs; season it and cover with a light crust; bake ¾ of an hour. Uncooked potatoes may be used in slices; put first a layer of them, then a layer of meat or fish; add butter, and season with onion, catsup or pickles; pour over two beaten eggs; lay on upper crust; bake 1 hour.

No. 150.

POTATO BISCUITS.

Peel and steam 4 good-sized potatoes; mash them and pour in a mortar; moisten with a little raw egg; then add loaf sugar to make them sweet; beat the whites of 4 eggs to a snow and mix with the potatoes; add a tablespoonful of orange flower water; place on paper so as to form either round or oblong biscuits; bake slowly till of a fine color; remove paper when done.

No. 151.

BAKED APPLE PUDDING.

Put in a well-buttered pan a layer of breadcrumbs, then a layer of apples cut small; a sprinkling of grocer's currants, some brown sugar; repeat this process till pan is full; then pour over melted butter; finish by putting breadcrumbs on top. Bake 1 hour.

No. 152.

APPLE OMELETTE.

Peel apples; take out cores; cut them in thin slices and dip in brandy, and dust over finely-grated lemon peel; put in frying-pan of boiling lard; shake a few minutes over a lively fire, and take them up; beat some eggs; sweeten to taste; stir in the fruit and fry. When done, double up the omelette, dust it with sifted sugar, and, if possible, glaze it.

No. 153.

SWISS APPLE PIE.

Peel, core, and quarter some apples. Boil the peel and the cores with a few cloves in ½ pint of water, and sugar enough to sweeten it. Lay the apples in a pie-dish, mixing with them ¼ pound grocer's currants which have been washed and dried in a cloth. Add to the liquor a glass of red wine and the grated rinds and juice of two lemons. Put this over the apples; slice in 2 ounces of butter; line the edges and top with light tart paste; bake 1 hour. When done, sift powdered loaf sugar on crust.

No. 154.

PUDDING A LA MODE.

Take ½ dozen good-sized apples; peel, core, and cut into quarters; boil in very little water till soft; mash them to a pulp, with grated rind and juice of a lemon; beat up the yolks of 4 and the whites of 2 eggs; add 2 sponge-cakes soaked in raisin-wine, 6 ounces of butter just melted over the fire; mix the whole together. Line the pudding-dish with a light butter-paste. Bake 1 hour, and turn out to serve.

No. 155.

APPLE CAKE.

Take 1 pound pulped apples, 1 pound flour, ½ pound sugar, ½ pound melted butter, powdered cinnamon, 6 eggs well beaten and strained, 2 ounces candied citron-chips, and 4 spoonfuls ale-yeast. Knead it well, let rise, put in mould, and bake in quick oven. After cake has risen, add currants if needed.

No. 156.

PUDDING A LA MARINIERE.

Half pound each of flour and beef-suet, ¼ pound currants, and 4 eggs. Mix it into a paste with a little water, and roll it out flat; then empty a small preserving-pot of apple-jam in the middle; fasten up to make a round pudding; tie in cloth; boil 1 hour.

No. 157.

FISH PUDDING.

Line a small dish with a thin, yet rich, paste, and fill with small collops of boned fish, with bruised bay-leaf, chopped parsley, onion, pepper, fish-sauce. Put on top crust, tie in cloth, and boil according to size of pudding.

No. 158.

APPLE STUFFING.

Take a good half pound of the pulp of tart apples, which have either been baked or scalded; add 2 ounces of bread crumbs, some powdered sage, onion, and season it with cayenne pepper. This is a fine stuffing for roast geese, ducks, pork, etc.

No. 159.

APPLE JAM.

Pare and core 2 dozen full-grown apples; put in a saucepan with water enough to cover them; boil to a pulp, mash with a spoon till smooth, and to every pint of fruit put half pound of white sugar; boil again 1 hour; skim, if necessary. When cold put in preserving jars.

No. 160.

BAKED APPLE DUMPLINGS.

Make a rich paste with butter and flour, peel some apples, stick 3 or 4 cloves in each, and cover the fruit entirely with paste. If the oven is too hot they will burn outside. When done sift fine white sugar over and serve hot.

No. 161.

POTATO PUDDING.

Boil 1 pound of potatoes, mash while hot, stir in 3 ounces fresh butter, 2 ounces of pounded loaf sugar, rind and juice of half a lemon, and a little cream; butter a dish, lay all into it, and bake 30 minutes in a moderately hot oven; the yolks of 4 raw eggs may be added, and brandy or Madeira used instead of lemon juice—or 1 pound of currants can be added. This pudding can be boiled or baked; if boiled serve with wine sauce, if baked use thin puff paste to line and cover dish.

No. 162.

PUDDING A LA FECULE DES POMMES DE TERRE.

Bruise a couple of bay leaves and boil them in 1 pint of water or milk; mix two dessertspoonfuls of potato flour and powdered loaf sugar; when smooth pour over them the hot liquid, stirring all the time. Put in a buttered dish, bake quarter of an hour in a hot oven; when done pour over a half pint of cream. If to be eaten cold pour on fresh cream before sending up; strew crushed loaf sugar on top.

No. 163.

POTATOES IN MEAT PUDDINGS AND PIES.

It has been found that there is a general improvement in meat puddings and pies when potatoes are used with them. They seem to take away much of the overrichness and renders them much more palatable.

No. 164.

STUFFED POTATOES.

Wash and peel five large-sized potatoes, scoop them out hollow from one end to the other, and fill this opening with sausage or forcemeat, then dip the potatoes in melted butter and put them on a baking-dish. Let them bake in a moderately hot oven about 30 or 40 minutes; serve just as soon as done. You can use sauce with them if you choose.

No. 165.

CURRIED POTATOES.

Curry the potatoes by slicing them, raw or cold boiled, frying them in butter; mixing curry powder in gravy, stewing them a little. Little pieces of ham should be stuck over the surface of the potatoes when put on a dish. Lemon juice or pickles can be added.

No. 166.

SWEET POTATOES BAKED OR ROASTED.

Peel and put on a roaster beneath the meat or in a dripping-pan, besides turning them now and then so as to brown evenly. Place them in the oven when the meat is nearly done, so that both may be served and ready at the same time.

No. 167.

POTATO SOUFFLEE.

One pint cream, boiled; mix 2 tablespoonfuls of potato flour with the yolks of 4 eggs, add 1 ounce butter, 2 ounces powdered loaf sugar, lemon peel; pour cream over all. Put in a stewpan on the fire; keep stirring and take off just as it comes to a boil. Let it get cold, then mix in it 6 yolks of eggs; beat 6 whites to a snow, stir them in lightly, place on dish and put in oven till properly risen. Serve in same dish; can be flavored with chocolate.

No. 168.

POTATOES AND KIDNEY.

Take a sheep's kidney, or piece of calf's liver of same size, chop and season with salt, spices, and a few herbs, chopped; add 2 ounces fresh butter in small pieces, chop 4 good-sized potatoes (raw), washed and peeled, and mix with the meat. Put all on baking-dish, sift crumbs over it, bake ¾ hour in slow oven. Serve on same dish. A little onion may be added.

No. 169.

POTATO PATTIES.

Butter the pans, strew breadcrumbs over the insides and fill with nicely mashed potatoes flavored with mushroom catsup, grated lemon peel, savory herbs, chopped; add olive oil or fresh butter, sift over more breadcrumbs; place in oven till brown, take out of pans and serve. Very thin puff paste may line the pans instead of the breadcrumbs.

No. 170.

WHOLE BONED HAM.

Take a ham, split it down on the inside, not through the skin, as that must not be broken; but cut it down on the side that goes next to the dish. Take out all the bone. One can mushrooms, half-sized can truffles, 1 small clove of garlic, 2 stalks celery, teaspoonful of thyme; chop this all up, not very fine, and put this stuffing where the bone has been taken out; sew the ham up and put it in a close bag so it will keep its shape. Put in the pot 1 dozen cloves and let ham boil slowly 3 hours; when done put in a close pan to press till very cold. Take skin off; 1½ pints of ham water, 1½ pints of any soup stock, 1 box gelatine dissolved in a cup of cold water; put all these together, add pepper and salt, beat up whites and shells of 2 eggs and put in the stock and ham water to clear it. Put all on the fire and stir till it boils; do not allow any fat to come on it; skim it well; strain the jelly through a flannel bag after boiling 10 minutes. If you have no ham mould take some jelly, cut in diamond shape, and put around the dish, and the rest cut fine and put all over the ham. Garnish your dish with carrots, beets cut into flower forms, parsley, a little here and there on either side of the ham.

No. 171.

WHOLE CHICKEN IN GLACEE.

Take out all the bones in a medium-sized chicken; ¼ pound ham, ½ pound veal, ½ can mushrooms, ¼ can truffles, small piece of onion, a little thyme and parsley. Chop the meat, parsley, thyme, celery, very fine together. Cut the mushrooms in slices; skin the truffles and cut them and put these into the chopped meat; pepper and salt to taste. Where the bones have been taken out stuff tightly with this stuffing; pepper and salt to taste. Tie it in a bag tightly. When done press it over night under a heavy press. Next morning take it out; cut off each end and put it into either a melon mould or charlotte mould. Now take 3 pints of the chicken water, skim off all the grease, put salt and pepper and nutmeg in it. Melt 1 box of gelatine in cold water; take 2 whites of eggs with their shells and put all in chicken water. Put on fire; stir it; let it boil 10 minutes. Strain through a flannel bag. Let it get nearly cold— enough to be dipped up with a spoon. Boil hard 2 eggs; cut the eggs in 6 slices; 1 sprig of parsley in center of egg and put at 4 sides of the chicken with parsley turned down. Pour the jelly all over it; put in ice-box to get cold. Turn it out of mould and garnish dish with water-cresses or celery, frizzed. Duck in glacee can be put up in the same way.

No. 172.

DEVILED CRABS.

Take 1½ dozen crabs; boil them done; pick them carefully out of shell; take ½ dozen crackers; 1 pint of milk is poured over the crackers, mashed fine. Strain the crackers through a fine sieve. Beat up 3 eggs light, and put into the strained crackers salt and cayenne pepper (strong); nutmeg to taste. Now put the crab meat in this. Wash the crab shells clean and wipe perfectly dry. One and one-half dozen will make 1 dozen crabs. Brown to a handsome shade 2 crackers. Mash them fine and put them through a sieve. Put a tablespoonful of wine in the crab meat. Fill the shells; over each crab sift some of this brown cracker dust. Ten minutes before the time for serving put in a quick oven. Lay a napkin on your dish; put them on the napkin and lay parsley round them. Serve perfectly hot.

No. 173.

OX TONGUE GLACEE.

Put the tongue to soak over night. Steady boil for 2½ hours. Take out of pot and take root off of it before it gets cold. Then let it get cool. Skin it and cut it in slices. Make the jelly as directed to make chicken jelly. Let it get cool enough to work. Take 2 jelly moulds; put a layer of jelly just stiff enough on the bottom of moulds; then a layer of tongue; then a layer of jelly and continue till moulds are full. This quantity will fill the two moulds. Put on ice and let it get cold. This is served with salad with Mayonnaise dressing.

No. 174.

PICKLED OYSTERS.

Take 50 large oysters, ½ pint of the liquor, ½ pint of vinegar, 1 tablespoonful of allspice and cloves mixed, ½ dozen leaves of mace, salt to taste, cayenne pepper. Put the liquor and vinegar on the fire. As soon as this boils drop a few oysters in at a time and let them stay just long enough to curl, not over two minutes. Put the oysters, as soon as taken out, in a jar. When all have been taken out, pour the liquor on them and cover up tightly.

No. 175.

RED CABBAGE PICKLE.

Cut the cabbage up in slices, sprinkle salt over it, for 3 days set it in the sun or warm place; ½ pint of vinegar and ½ gallon of water put on to boil together; pour this on the cabbage and let it soak for 1 day. When it feels crisp and the salt is out, take 2 tablespoonfuls each of mustard and celery seed, horseradish grated, 1 tablespoonful of brown sugar, pepper and salt to taste, 1 quart of vinegar, teaspoonful tamarack, 3 small white onions cut up fine. Mix all together and put in a pot and then pour the boiling vinegar, with sugar and tamarack, over the cabbage. Then fasten up in jars tightly, and in a few weeks this will be ready for use.

No. 176.

PEACH MARMALADE.

Take soft peaches. One-half pound of peaches to ½ pound of sugar. Peel the peaches over night and sprinkle the sugar over them. The peaches must not be cling-stone. Next morning pour all the juice off and put the juice in a kettle and let it get hot, then put in the peaches, nutmeg, cloves, allspice to taste. When it boils, stir and mash them up well. Let boil slowly for 1½ hours. When thick enough, put into pots, without covering them, till next day. Put a little brandy over them and seal up tightly.

No. 177.

QUINCE PRESERVES.

One peck quinces; peel, core, and weigh them. It will require just so many pounds of sugar. Put on the peelings of the quinces and let them boil perfectly done. Then put the preserves in and the rind of 4 lemons. Let all boil ¼ hour, till soft enough to allow a straw to pass partly through them. One-half pint of water (quite clean and clear) to 1 pound of sugar; make a syrup and let it commence to boil; skim it and then put in the fruit. Let the fruit boil ½ hour exactly; then take out the fruit and lay on a dish. Let your syrup boil steadily ¾ hour longer. Put your jars in hot water on the stove. Put the fruit in them clear of syrup. Then pour in the syrup and stop the jars up tightly while standing in the boiling water. Let them stand in ¼ hour.

No. 178.

BEEF A LA MODE.

Take 10 pounds of beef, tie it up perfectly round with strings and skewers; take a tablespoonful of butter and put it in a pot large enough to hold the beef, put the meat in it and let it come to a light brown; 1 bunch of carrots, ½ bunch of thyme; cut the carrots up into large quarters; 3 turnips cut into 4 quarters, 3 onions peeled and stuck full of cloves, ½ bunch each of parsley and celery tops; cover the meat in the pot with water, and put in all the vegetables; let them boil slowly 1 hour with salt and pepper; make the liquor as thick as gravy, then let it boil 1½ hours longer; put in two medium-sized pickles sliced in four quarters; before dishing up put in wine-glass of wine; when ready to go to the table put the vegetables all around the dish, and send the sauce up in a sauce-bowl; if the meat should be tough let it boil 1 hour longer.

No. 179.

GOOSE PORK.

Take a fresh ham, score the skin nicely; take the inside of a loaf of bread, ½ can of mushrooms, 1 onion, ½ bunch of parsley, not quite ½ bunch of thyme, nearly ½ bunch of sage; cut the parsley and onion very fine, also the mushrooms; rub the thyme and sage together very fine; 1 tablespoonful of butter must be put in the breadcrumbs, and all the above must be mixed up well with it; make 5 or 6 pockets in the ham, stuff this dressing tightly in them, tie a string around them to keep the dressing in, put pepper and salt on it and dust over a little flour. Put the ham in a dressing-pan in an oven, baking slowly for 4 hours. Be sure to baste and dust it well with flour until done. When done take all fat off of gravy, which if not thick enough must be thickened. Boil rice enough to garnish the dish with, boiling in half milk and half water; when done let it get cool, beat 2 eggs, pepper and salt, a little of the mushroom water, 1 tablespoonful of sugar; put these in rice, roll out in croquettes, put them first in beaten egg and then in breadcrumbs; fry a light brown. Make apple sauce and serve with it.

No. 180.

YOUNG BROILED CHICKENS.

Take spring chickens, dress them well, split them down the back, broil without burning, baste with butter and cream, replace on gridiron and let broil a little more, and the essence left from basting will be the gravy to put over them. Season with salt and pepper. When done, cut in 4 parts; place in a dish and garnish with parsley. Serve with salad with Mayonnaise dressing.

No. 181.

BROILED QUAILS.

Take quails and serve as the spring chicken, only use currant jelly with the cream and butter. Serve as above.

No. 182.

FRICASSEE RABBIT.

Clean a rabbit, cut in 4 quarters, pepper, salt and flour it, fry a delicate brown, dust flour in frying-pan; cut in it, very fine, 1 small onion, and parsley, ½ pint each of milk and and cream, and pour in frying-pan; then put rabbit in to stay ¼ hour. Boil rice dry and put it round the dish with rabbit and gravy in the center.

EASTER HAM.

Take a smoked ham, make pockets in it; take ¼ peck cabbage sprouts, 1 bunch celery, chop them up fine. Skin the ham and stuff the pockets with the above, then put the skin on again. The pockets should not be cut till the skin is taken off, because that must be kept whole. Tie up in a bag which fits the ham, let 2½ hours be the time for boiling it; when done, take out of bag, take off the skin, stick in top of the ham 2 dozen cloves. Baste with a little melted sugar and sift some fine breadcrumbs over it; put in oven to get a light brown. Serve it with cabbage sprouts or cauliflower.

No. 184.

VENISON CUTLETS.

Give the cutlets the shape of a ham; broil them on a gridiron. Take 1 tumbler currant jelly, 1 tablespoonful butter, 1 wineglass of wine, salt and pepper to taste and make a hot sauce. Heat the dish to put the cutlets on, and pour the sauce over them. Serve hot. Serve Saratoga potatoes with it, placing them in center of dish.

No. 185.

HICKORY-NUT CAKE.

Mix 4 cups flour, 2 of sugar, 1 of butter, 2 teaspoonfuls cream tartar, all together; dissolve 1 teaspoonful of carbonate of soda in a cup of milk and mix this with the first. Add 1 pint of nut meats.

No. 186.

DELMONICO'S PUDDING.

One quart milk with ½ teaspoonful salt; set this on the fire to boil; mix 3 tablespoonfuls of corn-starch with a little cold milk and stir in just before the milk boils. Boil 5 minutes. To 6 tablespoonfuls, sugar beat the yolks of 3 eggs and add any flavoring extract; pour the corn-starch, while hot, into this, then whip the whites of 3 eggs and drop it on top of pudding in form of kisses, and brown in the oven.

No. 187.

CHRISTMAS PLUM PUDDING.

Chop fine ½ pound beef suet. Stone and chop 1 pound raisins; wash and pick 1 pound currants. Soak the crumbs of a small loaf of bread in 1 pint of milk; when it has taken up all the milk, add to it the raisins, currants, and suet, 2 eggs well beaten, a tablespoonful of sugar, a wineglassful of brandy, the grating of 1 nutmeg, and other spices if desired. Boil 4 hours. For a sauce, beat ¼ pound butter to a cream with ½ pound powdered sugar and flavor with brandy.

No. 188.

ORANGE PUDDING.

Make the same as lemon pudding, using orange instead of lemon.

No. 189.

PICKLED SALMON.

Boil a 6 or 7 pound salmon done; put it into an earthen jar, after taking all the bones out without breaking it; put pepper and salt on it; 1 pint of vinegar, 1 teaspoonful allspice, 2 dozen grains of cloves, ½ dozen grains of black pepper, little red pepper; put all these in the vinegar and let come to a boil. Put in also 3 leaves of mace. Pour it all over the salmon and cover over tight. If made in the morning it will be fit to eat in the evening. Sturgeon can be made in the same way.

No. 190.

BRANDIED PEACHES.

Take 9 pounds of Heath peaches, 7 pounds of loaf sugar, 1 quart of white brandy. Have a strong lye, hot, but not boiling, over the fire. Throw half a dozen peaches into it at a time; let them remain 4 minutes; take them out again and put them into cold water. Continue this till all are done. Then, with a coarse towel, rub them till perfectly smooth, and put them into another vessel of cold water. Make a syrup of the sugar with 2 pints of water and ½ the white of an egg. Skim the syrup perfectly clear. Take the peaches out of the water, wipe them dry, put them in the syrup, and boil them till a straw will pass through them, then take them out to cool. Boil the syrup ¼ hour; then put in the brandy while hot and mix thoroughly. Having placed your peaches in glass jars, pour the syrup over them while hot, and when cold paste paper over them to protect them. Will be fit for use in 3 months.

No. 191.

STUFFED EGGS.

Cut 10 hard-boiled eggs in half lengthwise, take out the yolks, pound them in a mortar, add breadcrumbs soaked in milk and ¼ pound fresh butter. Pound all together; add a little chopped onion, parsley, bruised pepper, and grated nutmeg; mix it with the yolks of two raw eggs; fill the halved whites with this forcemeat; lay the remainder at the bottom of dish and place the stuffed eggs around it. Put in an oven and brown nicely.

No. 192.

EGG POTAGE.

Beat the yolks of 10 eggs and half their bulk of rich gravy. When frothed, turn out on a plate and place them over a saucepan of boiling water till the eggs are well set and form a cream. Cut this in neat strips, place them in a tureen of savory consomme, and serve immediately.

No. 193.

STEWED MUSSELS.

Boil them from the shell; take the beard out and put them in the stewpan with some of the liquor in which they were boiled, strain it on them; add some cream or milk, a bit of butter, pepper, and salt; dredge over flour; stir with spoon; let simmer for 10 minutes. Serve hot, with toast.

No. 194.

PANNED OYSTERS.

Take 50 large oysters; rinse clean and let drain; put in stewpan with ¼ pound of butter, salt, red and black pepper to season. Put pan over fire, stirring while cooking. When oysters begin to shrink, take off of fire and serve at once in a covered dish well heated.

No. 195.

STEWED CLAMS.

Take 50 large sand clams from their shells; put them in their own liquor and water in equal parts nearly to cover them; put them in a stewpan over a gentle fire for ½ hour; take off all scum; add I teacup butter, in which is worked 1 tablespoonful of flour, and pepper to taste. Cover stewpan and let simmer 15 minutes longer. Pour over toast. Milk can be used for water. Will taste better.

No. 196.

BROILED OYSTERS.

Take out the largest; lay them on a napkin to dry; then dip each in flour or cracker dust, or first in beaten egg; have a gridiron of coarse wire put over a bright fire; lay oysters on it; when one side is done turn over the other; put butter on a hot plate; sprinkle a little pepper over, and lay oysters on; serve with crackers.

No. 197.

CLAM CHOWDER.

Butter a basin and line it with grated breadcrumbs or soaked crackers; sprinkle pepper and bits of butter and finely-chopped parsley; put in a double layer of clams; season with pepper and bits of butter; another layer of soaked crackers; turn a plate over the basin and bake in a hot oven for ¾ of an hour; use ½ pound of soda biscuit, and ¼ of a pound of butter for 50 clams.

No. 198.

BROILED SHAD.

Split fish in two; lay on gridiron over hot fire; broil gently; put the inside to the fire first; have a dish ready with ¼ of a pound of sweet butter in it; also, 1 teaspoonful each of salt and pepper worked in it; when the fish is done on both sides lay on a dish; turn it often in the butter; cover over, and set dish where it will be hot till wanted.

No. 199.

CODFISH CAKES.

Boil soaked cod; chop it fine; put to it an equal quantity of potatoes boiled and mashed; moisten with beaten eggs or milk; a bit of butter and a little pepper; lay out in form of small round cakes; flour outside and fry in hot lard till brown; let lard be boiling hot when cakes are put in; brown both sides.

No. 200.

OYSTER CHOWDER.

Butter a two-quart tin basin; cover with soaked crackers, bits of butter; put in a double layer of oysters; sprinkle fine pepper over, finely chopped parsley; then put a layer of soaked crackers and bits of butter, as before; then another layer of oysters and seasoning, and lastly soaked crackers and butter and 1 pint of oyster liquor and milk or water.

No. 201.

BAKED SHAD.

Clean the shad; cut off the head; split it half way down the back; scrape inside clean. To make stuffing, cut 2 slices of baker's bread; spread each with butter and sprinkle on pepper and salt, pounded sage; moisten it with hot water; fill the inside of the fish with this; tie a cord around it to keep stuffing in; dredge outside with flour; stick bits of butter all over outside; mix one teaspoonful each of salt and pepper over surface; then lay fish on muffin ring in dripping pan; put in 1 pint of water to taste with; if this is used up while baking, add more hot water; bake 1 hour in quick oven; baste often. When the fish is done there should be ½ pint of gravy in pan; if not, add more hot water; dredge in a full teaspoonful of flour with a bit of butter, a lemon sliced thin; stir this smooth, then pour in gravy-boat; lay slices of lemon over fish and serve with mashed potatoes.

No. 202.

LOBSTER SAUCE.

Pick out the meat, boil down the shell, use the liquor for making the sauce with minced lobster, and buttered rolled flour. The berries may be used uncrushed.

No. 203.

OYSTER SAUCE.

Open the oysters, strain the liquor, put it in saucepan with butter rolled in flour; when melted add the oysters and a little cream. As soon as it boils add lemon juice; beaten mace and white pepper may be used.

No. 204.

SOFT CLAMS FRIED.

Take them from the shell, wash them in plenty of water, lay on a napkin to dry. Roll in flour very thickly; have a frying-pan one-third full of hot lard, a tablespoonful of salt to 1 pound of lard; lay the clams in with a fork one at a time; lay close together, and fry gently till brown on one side, then turn them over and let the other side brown. Place in hot dish ready for table.

No. 205.

CRABS DRESSED COLD.

Pick out all the flesh, mix it with oil, vinegar, cayenne pepper, and some yolks of hard boiled eggs; put all this in the shell, then on a dish with fresh herbs and lettuce around it—fresh water-cresses will do to decorate with.

No. 206.

LOBSTER SALAD.

Pick out all the flesh from the lobster, taking care of the coral, if any; cut up the meat, not very small, put it in a salad dish, add anchovy, a few olives, chopped pickles, quartered hard boiled eggs, lettuce torn but not cut up; just before serving pour over the dressing; stew coral on top; sliced cucumber and an onion might be added.

The dressing is prepared in this way: Beat well the yolks of two fresh eggs and stir in one half teaspoonful of salt, 4 teaspoonfuls of mixed mustard, a pinch of cayenne pepper; add olive oil a little at a time, stirring all the while with a silver fork till it becomes stiff and flaky—it requires a half pint of oil—add 2 tablespoonfuls of vinegar; don't pour in more than a teaspoonful of oil at once. This quantity of dressing will do for 5 or 6 pounds of lobster.

No. 207.

FISH IN JELLY.

Make jelly by boiling down fish of any kind or calves' feet; clear it with white of egg, and pour a little milk in a mould. When jelly is set, put the prepared fish on it, and pour in more jelly till the mould is filled. When congealed, put a hot cloth round it for a little while, and turn it out on a dish. Serve for supper or luncheon.

No. 208.

DEVILED FISH.

Any kind of fish will do. Soak it for half an hour in vinegar, catsup, or any stock sauce. Drain and boil them, and serve with horseradish or mustard-sauce. You may roll your fish in curry powder if you wish.

No. 209.

FISH IN BATTER.

Rub some slices of fish in spices or shred herbs; then dip in batter, and fry brown.

No. 210.

FISH SANDWICHES.

Butter both sides of slices of bread. Upon half of their number lay thin fillets of anchovy, sardine, smoked salmon, or any other fish; sprinkle seasoning on top, and put the other slices on them. Lay the sandwiches on a dish, and place in oven till brown. The soft roe of shad or herring spread between bread and butter is good.

No. 211.

FISH PATTIES.

Use light paste. Have the large oysters. Make them hot by putting them in cream or a little butter, mixed with oyster liquor and delicate seasoning. Thicken with yolk of egg, and put in crust already baked in patty-pans. Take flesh from the tail part of cray-fish or lobsters; cut in slices. For salmon patties scrape the flesh with a knife, season with cayenne pepper; mix with a little butter or cream and yolk of egg, and shake it gently over the fire till done. Eels must be stewed in gravy, and the meat pounded in a mortar together with a little parsley and butter, and seasoning; warm it up with a glass of wine, and place in patty-crusts.

No. 212.

FISH SCALLOPED.

Beard the oysters and scallops; halve or quarter them; pack them in scallop-shells or small tins. Lay pieces of butter on them, and bake till brown on top. Serve them in the shells. Thin slices of salmon, pike, or turbot serve in same way. Squeeze lemon-juice over, to serve.

No. 213.

FISH, BOILED.

Place the fish in salted water, cold, if the fish is large, and hot if small sized. In the latter case, 2 or 3 minutes in boiling water will be enough; and a sheep's-head of 4 or 5 pounds will not require more than 10 minutes from the time the water boils. Use a strainer to place fish in saucepan. Salmon and all dark-fleshed fish require more boiling than white-fleshed kinds. Vinegar must be rubbed on the outside of fish before it is boiled; this keeps the skin from cracking. Serve boiled fish upon a napkin.

No. 214.

FISH, SALTED.

If your are to salt your fish never wash or wet it, but split open the larger fish, and remove the heads and intestines of the others, after scraping them; then pack them in a pickle-tub with finely powdered salt between each layer. The fish must be well covered on the top with salt.

No. 215.

FISH, CURRIED

A curry of lobster, shrimps, prawns, or crayfish is easily prepared. Take enough of the meat of either and rub it in curry powder. Have boiling gravy ready in a saucepan to make sauce for fish; when it boils take it off the fire, and add bits of butter and beaten yolks of egg to thicken with.

No. 216.

ORDINARY OMELETTE.

Beat and strain your eggs, season them, and add 1 tablespoonful of water, milk, or stock to every 6 eggs. Let some butter or oil get hot in a frying-pan, and pour in the eggs. When omelette is set and of a pale brown color on the underside, take it up, fold it together lightly, and serve hot. Do not turn omelettes in the pan.

No. 217.

SARDINE OMELETTE.

Bone the preserved fish, cut in dice pieces, toss it in olive oil; prepare the eggs in the usual way, season them and pour them up on the fish in the pan; or, fry the eggs separately and place the fish on the omelette when it is ready.

No. 218.

BACON OMELETTE.

Mince some cold boiled bacon, and mix it with eggs which are spiced and well beaten, or take raw bacon, chop it, put in frying-pan till browned, then pour beaten eggs on it, or else place some bacon on eggs just poured in frying-pan. When set, fold the omelette and serve with tomato sauce in the dish.

No. 219.

APPLES AND RICE.

Boil ½ pound rice in 1 quart of new milk. At the same time put some preserved apples in the oven to get hot. When the rice is done arrange it around a dish; put the preserve in the center; dust some sugar over it, and garnish the rice with slices of candied lemon peel. Before serving lay some pieces of fresh butter upon it. Must be eaten warm.

No. 220.

CHARLOTTE DES POMMES.

Peel and slice some apples; take a loaf of fine white bread; free it of crust and cut it in thin slices well buttered. Fit them in a mould well buttered, and put in a layer of apples sprinkled with grated lemon; peel and sweeten them with brown sugar. Next place a slice of bread and butter till mould is full; squeeze in the juice of two lemons, and bake it for 1 hour. Turn it out and serve as you would cake.

No. 221.

RED APPLES IN JELLY.

Nice formed apples in a stewpan with water to cover them. Add a spoonful of powdered cochineal, and simmer gently. When done put in dessert dish; add white sugar and juice of 2 lemons for a syrup. When boiled to a jelly put it in the apples. Decorate dish with lemon-peel cut in slices.

No. 222.

APPLE CHOCOLATE.

Boil in 1 quart of new milk 1 pound scraped French chocolate and 6 ounces of white sugar. Beat the yolks of 6 eggs and the whites of 2. When the chocolate has come to a boil, take off of fire; add the eggs, stirring well. At the bottom of a deep dish place a good layer of pulped apple, sweetened to taste; season with cinnamon. Pour chocolate over it and place the dish on a saucepan of boiling water. When the cream is set firmly it is done. Sift powdered sugar over it, and glaze with a red hot shovel.

No. 223.

APPLE JELLY.

Peel and core fine flavored apples; cut in large pieces and boil in very little water. When done put through a hair sieve; press them so as to get all the juice. For every quart of jelly take 1 pound of white sugar; boil it in the water which was used for the fruit, and skin it. Add the juice of the apples with the juice of four oranges squeezed into each quart. Boil ½ hour and keep it ready for use.

No. 224.

OYSTERS A LA POULETTE.

Put 25 oysters or one quart on the fire in their own liquor. The moment it begins to boil turn it into a hot dish through a colander. Leave the oysters in the colander. Put into the saucepan 2 ounces of butter, and when it bubbles sprinkle 1 ounce of sifted flour; let it cook a minute without taking color; stir it well with a wire egg-whisk; then add, mixing in well, a cupful of the oyster liquor; take it from the fire; mix in the yolks of 2 eggs, a little salt, and a very little red pepper, 1 teaspoonful of lemon juice, 1 grating of nutmeg. Beat it well, and then return it to the fire to set the eggs, without allowing it to boil; then put the oysters in.

No 225.

TRUFFLED OYSTERS.

Four dozen large oysters, 1 can of truffles, 6 ounces of chicken, 3 ounces of fat salt pork, 5 eggs, flour, toast, red pepper. Mince and then pound to a paste the chicken and salt pork, add red pepper, a pinch of salt, and the truffles cut fine and mixed in; lay the oysters out on the napkin, insert a penknife at the edge and split each oyster up and down inside without making the opening too large, then push in the forcemeat. As the oysters are stuffed lay them in flour and then dip in beaten egg and drop a few at a time in hot lard, and fry three or four minutes. The lard should be deep enough to immerse them. When they are golden brown take them up, drain on paper and put on toast.

No. 226.

PHILADELPHIA STYLE OF COOKING CANVASBACK DUCK.

Draw the duck and sew up the incision tightly and closely, leaving one opening; through this fill the interior with red currant jelly and good port wine. Sew up and close the opening and roast the duck 20 minutes in a hot oven; by this process the jelly, the wine, and the natural juices off the duck combine and permeate the flesh, giving a most delicious result.

No. 227.

BROILED STUFFED OYSTERS.

Grate the yolks of hard-boiled eggs, 4 or 5 to every dozen of the largest oysters; mince half as much salt pork and mix in black pepper, chopped parsley, add a raw egg, the yolk to make a paste; split the inside by moving a penknife up and down without making a very large opening at the edge; add the stuffing, dip them in fine breadcrumbs, then into melted butter on a plate, then into breadcrumbs again, and broil them over a clear fire.

No. 228.

GAME SOUP.

Take all the meat off the breasts of any cold birds left from preceding day. Pound it in a mortar, beating to pieces the legs and bones, and boil them in some broth for an hour. Boil 6 turnips, mash them and strain through cloth with the pounded meat. Strain the broth and put a little of it at a time into the sieve to help you strain all of it through. Put soup kettle near the fire, but do not let it boil. When ready to dish your dinner, have 6 yolks of eggs mixed with ½ pint of cream; strain through a sieve; put soup on fire, and when coming to a boil put in eggs and stir well with wooden spoon. Do not let it boil, lest it curdle.

No. 229.

ARTICHOKES.

Soak them in cold water, wash them well, and put them in plenty of boiling water, with a handful of salt, and let them boil gently till they are tender, which will take 1½ to 2 hours. To know when they are done, draw out a leaf. Trim them and drain them on a sieve. Send up melted butter with them, which some put into small cups so that each guest may have one.

No. 230.

STEWED OYSTERS.

Large oysters will do for stewing. Stew a couple of dozen in their own liquor. When coming to a boil, skim well, take them up, beard them, strain the liquor through a sieve, and lay the oysters on a dish. Put an ounce of butter in a stewpan; when melted, put to it as much flour as will dry it up, the liquor of the oysters, 3 tablespoonfuls of milk or cream, a little white pepper, salt, a little catsup, chopped parsley, grated lemon peel and juice. Let it boil up for a couple of minutes till it is smooth, then take it off the fire, put in the oysters, and let them get warm. Line the sides and bottom of a hash-dish with bread sippets and pour your oysters and sauce into it.

No. 231.

FRICASSEED RABBIT.

Take a fine, fat rabbit, clean it well, salt and pepper it, put it in hot lard to fry to a pretty delicate brown; when done take out, pour out a portion of the grease, and cut up three onions, thicken with three tablespoonfuls of flour, stir well, pour on water enough to cover the rabbit, which is now put back in the skillet; cover it over and let boil for ¾ of an hour. Just before serving cut up a little parsley and put in; serve it with either roasted or fried potatoes.

No. 232.

COLD VEAL AND HAM TIMBALES.

Timbale paste, 1 pound of corned bacon, 2 pounds of leg veal, 6 hard boiled eggs, 1 teaspoonful each of celery salt and marjoram, 3 sprigs of parsley, white pepper and salt to taste; line the timbale mould with the paste, first setting it on a greased baking-pan; cut the ham and veal into scallops and the eggs into slices; with them make alternate layers with the seasonings; when all are used fill with water, wet the exposed edges of the paste cover, ornament the edges, and bake in a moderate oven 2 hours; when cold open the mould and serve as may be desired.

No. 233.

BEEFSTEAK AND OYSTERS.

Take a tender sirloin steak, put it in a hot skillet, let it fry 15 minutes; when done take the hearts out of 1 quart of oysters, and put the oysters in the skillet where the steak came out, sprinkle a little flour over them, a small piece of butter, a little of the oyster liquor, enough to make a nice gravy;

season to taste and a little nutmeg. Put steak on platter, pour this oyster gravy over them, and serve hot.

No. 234.

FRICASSEED CHICKEN.

ONE PAIR.

Cut a chicken in quarters, make a rich gravy of 1 pint of milk, 1 pint of water or oyster liquor, 3 tablespoonfuls of flour, a little butter mixed in the flour; after the chicken nearly boils in the milk and water, then put in the flour mixed with the butter; put in a few sprigs of parsley; let all boil till done. Boil some rice in a saucepan so as not to break up the grains; put the chicken when done on the platter, put the rice all round dish, pour the gravy in the center all over the chicken, and serve hot.

No. 235.

ROASTED LEG OF PORK, CALLED MOCK GOOSE.

Parboil it; take off the skin; then put it down to roast; baste it with butter, and make a powder of finely minced or dried powdered sage, black pepper, salt, and some breadcrumbs rubbed together through a colander. Add to this some finely minced onion; sprinkle it with this when almost roasted. Put ½ pint made gravy into the dish, and goose-stuffing under the knuckle-skin, or garnish the dish with balls of it fried or boiled.

No. 236.

KIDNEYS.

Cut them lengthwise, score them, sprinkle some pepper and salt on them, and run a wire skewer through them to keep them from curling on the gridiron, that they may broil evenly. Broil them over a clear fire, turning them often till done. This will take about 10 or 12 minutes if you have a brisk fire, or fry them in butter, and make a gravy in the pan after taking the kidneys out by putting in a teaspoonful of flour; as soon as it looks brown, put in as much water as will make gravy. It will take 5 minutes more to fry them than to broil them. A few parsley leaves chopped fine, and mixed with a little butter, pepper, and salt, may be put on each kidney.

No. 237.

STEAKS.

Cut the steaks rather thinner than for broiling. Put some butter into a frying-pan, and when it is hot lay in the steaks and keep turning them till they are done enough. By this means the meat will be more equally dressed and more evenly browned, and will be found to be much more relishing.

No. 238.

FISH TURBOT.

Boil a 5-pound of any firm fish not quite done; take it out and pick all bones out of it; then make a cream sauce for it. Having taken the hearts out of 1 pint of oysters, put them in the cream sauce; also ½ pint milk, 2 tablespoonfuls flour, 1 tablespoonful butter, 2 yolks of eggs. Let all boil together; then put the fish in it; season with pepper and salt to taste; put into a pudding-dish. Chop up a stalk of celery very fine, and put in it; sift some breadcrumbs over it, with small bits of butter. Put in oven and let bake ¾ hour. Garnish dish with fried oysters or fried potatoes.

No. 239.

TONGUE.

Tongue requires more cooking than a ham. One that has been salted and dried should be put to soak 24 hours before wanted, in plenty of water; a green one from the pickle needs soaking only a few hours. Put the tongue into plenty of cold water and let it be 1 hour gradually warming and give it from 3½ to 4 hours very slow simmering according to size.

No. 240.

HAM.

Give it plenty of water-room, and put it in while the water is cold; let it heat gradually and let it be on the fire 1½ hours before it comes to a boil; let it be well skimmed and keep it simmering very gently. A middle-sized ham will take from 4 to 5 hours according to its thickness.

No. 241.

FRIED PERCH.

Wipe the fish well, wipe them on a dry cloth, flour them lightly all over, and fry them 10 minutes in hot lard or drippings; lay them on a hair sieve. Send them up on a hot dish garnished with sprigs of parsley.

BREAD AND BUTTER PUDDING.

Have ready a quart dish; wash and pick 2 ounces of currants; strew a few at bottom of dish; cut about 4 layers of very thin bread and butter and between each layer strew some currants. Then break 4 eggs in a basin, leaving out 1 white; beat them well and add 4 ounces of sugar and a nutmeg; stir it well together with a pint of new milk; pour it over about 10 minutes before you put it in the oven. Bake ¾ hour.

No. 243.

PANCAKES AND FRITTERS.

Break 3 eggs in a basin, beat them up with a little nutmeg and salt; put to them 4½ ounces of flour and a little milk; beat to a smooth batter. Add, by degrees, milk enough to make the thickness of cream. Frying pan must be about the size of a pudding-plate and very clean or they will stick; make it hot and to each pancake put in a piece of butter as large as a walnut; when it is melted pour in the batter to cover the bottom of pan; make them the thickness of a half-dollar; fry a light brown on both sides.

Apple fritters can be made in the same way by adding 1 spoonful more of flour. Peel your apples and cut them in thick slices, take out core, dip them in the batter, fry in hot lard. Put on sieve to drain; grate loaf sugar over them.

No. 244.

BOSTON APPLE PUDDING.

Peel 1½ dozen good apples, take out cores, cut them small, put in stewpan that will just hold them with a little water, cinnamon, 2 cloves, and the peel of a lemon; stew over a slow fire till soft, then sweeten with moist sugar, and pass it through a fine sieve. Add to it the yolks of 4 eggs and 1 white, ¼ pound butter, half a nutmeg, a grated lemon peel, and juice of 1 lemon; beat all together; line inside of pie-dish with good paste; put in the pudding and bake half an hour.

No. 245.

SPRING FRUIT PUDDING.

Peel and wash 4 dozen sticks of rhubarb; put in stewpan with the pudding, a lemon, a little cinnamon, and enough moist sugar to make it sweet; set it over a fire and reduce it to a marmalade; pass through a hair sieve and go on as directed in the above receipt, leaving out lemon juice, as the rhubarb is acid enough.

No. 246.

NOTTINGHAM PUDDING.

Peel 6 apples, core them but leave the apples whole; fill up where you took out the core, with sugar. Place them in a pie-dish and pour over them a nice, light batter, prepared as for batter pudding; bake an hour in moderate oven.

No. 247.

MAIGRE PLUM PUDDING.

Simmer ½ pint of milk with 2 blades of mace, and a roll of lemon peel for 10 minutes, then strain it into a basin, set it away to get cold, then beat 3 eggs in a basin with 3 ounces of loaf sugar and the third of a nutmeg, then add 3 ounces of flour, beat it well together, and add the milk by degrees. Put in 3 ounces of fresh butter broken into small bits and 3 ounces of breadcrumbs, 3 ounces of currants washed and picked clean, 3 ounces of raisins stoned and chopped; stir it well together, butter a mould, put it in, and tie a cloth tight over it; boil 2½ hours, serve it with melted butter, 2 tablespoonfuls of brandy, and a little loaf sugar.

No. 248.

PLAIN BREAD PUDDING.

Put 5 ounces of breadcrumbs in a basin, pour ¾ pints of boiling milk over them, put a plate on the top to keep in the steam, let stand 20 minutes; then beat up quite smooth with it 2 ounces of sugar, and a saltspoon of nutmeg; break 4 eggs on a plate, leaving out 1 white, beat them well and add them to the pudding; stir it well together, and put it in a mould that has been well buttered and floured; tie a cloth over it and boil one hour.

No. 249.

FLEMISH WAFFLES.

One and one-half pints of flour, ½ teaspoonful of salt, 2 tablespoonfuls of sugar, 3 tablespoonfuls of butter, 1½ teaspoonfuls of baking powder, 4 eggs, ½ pint of thin cream, 1 teaspoonful each of the extract of cinnamon and vanilla; rub the butter and sugar to a cream, add the eggs one at a time, beating 3 or 4 minutes between each addition; sift flour, salt, and powder together, add these to the butter, etc., with the vanilla, cinnamon, and thin cream. Mix into batter as for griddle cakes, have waffle-iron hot and well greased, pour in batter enough to fill it two-thirds full, shut it up, and turn it over immediately; be careful not to get the iron too hot, as the waffles will only take from 4 to 5 minutes to cook. When done sift sugar over them and serve at once on a napkin.

No. 250.

SOFT WAFFLES.

One quart of flour, ½ teaspoonful of salt, 1 teaspoonful of sugar, 2 teaspoonfuls of baking powder, 1 large tablespoonful of butter, 2 eggs, 1½ pints of milk. Sift flour, powder, and salt together, rub in the butter cold, add the beaten eggs, mix into batter, have waffle-iron hot and well greased each time; fill two-thirds full and close it up; when brown turn over, sift sugar on them and serve hot.

No. 251.

CRANBERRY TART.

Pick and wash some cranberries in several waters, put them in a dish with the juice of half a lemon, quarter of a pound of loaf sugar crushed to 1 quart of cranberries; cover it with puff paste and bake it three-quarters of an hour. If tart paste is used take it from the oven five minutes before it is done and ice it; return it to the oven, and send to the table cold.

No. 252.

APPLE TART.

Pare, core, and quarter some apples; make an apple pie; then when pie is done cut out the whole of the center, leaving the edges; when cold pour on the apple some rich boiled custard, and placed round it some small leaves of puff paste of a light color.

No. 253.

GRAHAM MUFFINS.

One quart of Graham flour, 1 tablespoonful of brown sugar, 1 teaspoonful of salt, 3 teaspoonfuls of baking powder, 1 egg, and 1 pint of milk; sift the flour, sugar, salt, and powder together; add the beaten egg and milk, mix into a batter, fill cold well-greased muffin pans two-thirds full; bake 15 minutes in hot oven.

No. 254.

YORKSHIRE PUDDING.

[Under Roast Beef.]

This pudding is to accompany a sirloin of beef, loin of veal, or any fat, juicy joint. Six tablespoonfuls of flour, 3 eggs, 1 tablespoonful of salt, 1 pint of milk so as to make a tolerably stiff batter, a little stiffer than for pancakes; beat it up well—it must not be lumpy; put a dish under the meat and let the drippings drop into it till it is quite hot and well greased, then pour in the batter; when the upper surface is brown and set, then turn it over that both sides may brown alike. If you wish it to cut firm and the pudding an inch thick, it will take two hours at a good fire.

No. 255.

CORN BREAD.

One pound of cornmeal well sifted, mixed with boiling water or milk to the consistency of a moderate batter; then beat 4 eggs, putting the yolks in the batter, and the whites must be beaten up to a froth and put in just before baking; salt to taste; put in a baking-pan and bake quickly in a hot oven; a tablespoonful of butter or lard is also mixed with the meal.

No. 256.

FRENCH MUFFINS.

One and a half pints flour, 1 cupful honey, ½ teaspoonful salt, 2 teaspoonfuls baking-powder, 2 tablespoonfuls butter, 3 eggs, and little over ½ pint of milk or thin cream. Sift together the flour, salt, and powder; rub in the butter, cold; add the beaten eggs, milk or thin cream, and honey. Mix smoothly into a batter as for pound cake; about half fill sponge-cake tins, cold and carefully greased, and bake in good, steady oven 7 or 8 minutes.

No. 257.

BOSTON BROWN BREAD.

One half pint of flour, 1 pint cornmeal, ½ pint rye flour, 2 potatoes, 1 teaspoonful salt, 1 tablespoonful brown sugar, 2 teaspoonfuls baking-powder, ½ pint water. Sift the flour, cornmeal, rye flour, sugar, salt, and powder together. Peel, wash, and well boil two mealy potatoes; rub them through a sieve, thinning with water. When cold, use it to mix the flour, etc., into a batter like cake. Pour it into a greased mould, with a cover; place it in a saucepan half full of boiling water, when the loaf will simmer 1 hour without letting the water get into it. Remove, then take off the cover, and finish cooking it by baking in a fairly hot oven 30 minutes.

No. 258.

APPLE POT-PIE.

Fourteen apples peeled, cored, and sliced; 1½ pints flour, 1 teaspoonful baking-powder, 1 cupful sugar, ½ cupful butter, 1 cupful milk, large pinch of salt. Sift the flour with the powder and salt; rub in the butter, cold; add the milk, and mix into a dough as for tea-biscuits; with it line a shallow stewpan to within two inches of the bottom. Pour in 1½ cupfuls water, the apples and sugar; wet the edges, and cover with the rest of the dough; then place it in a moderate oven till the apples are cooked; then remove it from the oven; cut the top crust in four equal parts; dish the apples; lay on them the pieces of side crust cut in diamonds, and the pieces of top crust on a plate. Serve with cream.

No. 259.

OATMEAL CRACKNELS.

One and a half pints fine oatmeal, ½ pint Graham flour, 1 teaspoonful salt, 1 teaspoonful baking-powder, 1 pint of milk. Mix oatmeal and milk; let it stand, to swell, 5 hours in a cold place. Sift together the Graham flour, salt, and powder. Add it to the oatmeal; mix into a smooth dough. Flour the board with cornmeal; turn out dough, and roll ¼ inch thick; cut it out with cutter; lay them on greased baking tins; wash over with milk, and bake 10 minutes in moderate oven.

No. 260.

GERMAN WAFFLES.

One quart of flour, ½ teaspoonful salt, 3 tablespoonfuls sugar, 2 tablespoonfuls baking-powder, 2 tablespoonfuls lard, the rind of 1 lemon grated, 1 teaspoonful extract of cinnamon, 4 eggs, 1 pint thin cream. Sift flour, sugar, salt, and powder together; rub in lard, cold; add the beaten eggs, lemon rind, extract, and milk. Mix into smooth batter, rather thick. Bake in hot waffle-iron. Serve with sugar flavored with lemon.

No. 261.

TEA BISCUITS.

One quart of flour, 1 teaspoonful salt, ½ teaspoonful sugar, 2 teaspoonfuls baking-powder, 1 teaspoonful lard, 1 pint milk. Sift together flour, salt, powder, sugar; rub in lard, cold; add the milk, and form into a smooth, consistent dough. Flour the board; turn out the dough; roll it out to the thickness of ¾ of an inch; cut with a small round cutter; lay them close together on a greased baking-tin; wash over with milk. Bake in hot oven 20 minutes.

No. 262.

RICE MUFFINS.

Two cupfuls of cold boiled rice, 1 pint of flour, 1 teaspoonful of salt, 1 tablespoonful of sugar, 1½ teaspoonfuls of baking powder, ½ pint of milk, 3 eggs; thin out the rice with the milk and beaten eggs; sift the flour, sugar, salt and powder together; add the rice; mix into a smooth batter; fill muffin pans two-thirds full, having carefully greased them; bake 15 minutes in a hot oven.

No. 263.

CHEESE CRACKERS.

One and a half pints of flour, ½ pint of cornmeal, 1 teaspoonful of salt, 1 teaspoonful of baking-powder, 1 tablespoonful of butter, little more than ½ pint of milk; sift together flour, cornmeal, salt and powder; rub in the butter cold; add the milk; mix into a smooth, rather firm dough; flour the board; turn out the dough; give it a roll or two quickly, and roll it to the thickness of a quarter of an inch; cut out with a large round cutter; glaze the top as you would pies, and sprinkle cheese and cayenne pepper over top and bake ten minutes in hot oven; cheese straws can be made nearly the same way out of puff paste cut thin about ¼ of a yard long.

No. 264.

FRUIT JELLY.

Two pints of water; ½ pint of milk, and 1 gill of wine, 1 gill of lemon juice, the peel of 3 lemons, 1 pound of sugar, whites of 3 eggs beaten, not stiff, and stir in the above; melt and put in this 1 paper of gelatine; put on the fire and stir till it begins to boil; then stop for 10 minutes; take off; strain through a flannel bag, place in pan till cool enough to dip up with a spoon; peel and quarter in layers 1 orange; put a slim layer of jelly in bottom of mould; on this put 6 pieces of orange; now cover with jelly; second layer, drop 7 or 8 candied cherries on the top of layer in mould, another layer of jelly; then 5 or 6 Malaga grapes between them; 5 or 6 blanched almonds, a layer of jelly; on this candied cherries and almonds between them; then fill mould up with jelly; put on ice.

No. 265.

FROZEN PEACH CUSTARD.

One quart of milk; 5 yolks of eggs, 3 whites; boil milk; make a custard of it; sweeten to taste; cut in thin slices soft peaches; put peaches in custard when cold; freeze it for use; this can be moulded in form of a brick.

No. 266.

SNOWBALL.

Six apples, peeled and cored, ½ pound of rice washed well; put apples in pudding cloth; pour rice on top; leave room to swell; boil in pot 1½ hours; make wine sauce for it; this is a dinner dish.

No. 267.

BLANC-MANGE.

Take 1 package of gelatine, divide it in half; take 3 half pints of milk, 3 yolks of eggs; put on the milk to boil and make a custard of it; season to taste with lemon; melt one half of the gelatine, and melt it in ½ teacup of cold milk; then stir it in custard when done; take another 3 half pints of milk; let it boil; season with vanilla; sweeten to taste; melt the remaining half of the gelatine in a little milk and stir it in this last custard while it is hot; put out to cool enough, so it will mould; then take the first custard made and put in the mould, then on top of that in the same mould the last custard made; place on ice to cool; eat with whipped cream, seasoned with lemon or vanilla.

No. 268.

COFFEE BLANC-MANGE.

Take and divide 1 package of gelatine in half; take 1 pint of milk, ½ pint of coffee and let it boil; melt one half of the gelatine in a little milk; stir it in the boiled milk; now take 3 half pints of milk, stir in 2 tablespoonfuls of chocolate and boil it; take the remaining half of the gelatine, melt it in a little milk; stir it in the chocolate; let it get cold before putting in the mould; then put in the mould the portion made first, then the second portion on top of this; set away to cool; eat with whipped cream.

No. 269.

FRENCH COFFEE.

Three pints of water to 1 cup of ground coffee. Put the coffee grounds in a bowl, pour over it about ½ pint of cold water, and let stand for 15 minutes; bring remaining 2½ pints water to a boil. Take coffee in bowl, strain through a fine sieve, then take a French coffee pot, put coffee grounds in strainer at top of French pot, leaving the water in the bowl. Then take the boiling water and pour over the coffee very slowly; then set the coffee pot on the stove for five minutes; must not boil. Take off and pour in the cold water from the bowl that coffee was first soaked in to settle. Serve in another pot. The French have the reputation of making the best coffee. Use 3 parts Java and 1 part Mocha.

No. 270.

BISCUIT GLACE.

One and a half pints of cream, 12 ounces sugar, 8 yolks of eggs, 1 tablespoonful extract of vanilla; take 6 ounces crisp macaroons, pound in a mortar to dust; stir into the macaroon dust another tablespoonful extract of vanilla. Mix the cream, sugar, eggs, and extract. Place on the fire and stir this until it begins to thicken. Strain and rub through a hair sieve into a basin; put in freezer, and when nearly frozen mix in the macaroon dust and finish the freezing.

No. 271.

NOYEAU CORDIAL.

To 1 gallon of proof spirits add 3 pounds of loaf sugar and a tablespoonful of extract of almonds. Mix well together, and allow to stand 48 hours, covered closely; now strain through thick flannel and bottle. This liquor is much improved by adding ½ pint of apricot or peach juice.

No. 272.

RED CURRANT FRUIT-ICE.

Put 2 pints ripe currants, 1 pint red raspberries, ½ pint water in a basin. Place on the fire and allow to simmer a few minutes, then strain through a hair sieve. To this add 12 ounces of sugar and ½ pint of water. Place all into a freezing-can and freeze.

TOUTES FRUITS ICE-CREAM.

Take 2 quarts richest cream and add to it 1 pound pulverized sugar and 4 whole eggs. Mix all together; place on the fire, stirring constantly, and bring just to the boiling point; remove immediately and continue to stir till nearly cold; flavor this with 1 tablespoonful of extract of vanilla; place in freezer and freeze, after which mix thoroughly into it 1 pound of preserved fruit in equal parts of peaches, apricots, gages, cherries, pineapple, etc. All of these fruits are to be cut up into small pieces and well mixed with the cream, frozen. Should you wish to mould this ice, sprinkle it with a little carmine dissolved in a teaspoonful of water with 2 drops of spirits of ammonia. Mix in this color so that it will be streaky or in veins like marble.

No. 274.

CRUSHED STRAWBERRY ICE-CREAM.

Three pints best cream, 12 ounces pulverized white sugar, 2 whole eggs, 2 tablespoonfuls extract of vanilla. Mix all together in a porcelain-lined basin; place on the fire; stir constantly to the boiling point. Remove and strain through a hair sieve. Place in a freezer and freeze. Take 1 quart ripe strawberries, select, hull and put in a bowl; add 6 ounces pulverized sugar, white, and crush all down to a pulp; add this pulp to the frozen cream and mix in well. Now give the freezer a few additional turns to harden.

No. 275.

PEACH ICE-CREAM.

One dozen best, ripest red-cheeked peaches; peel and stone; place in china basin and crush with 6 ounces pulverized sugar. Take 1 quart best cream, 8 ounces pulverized sugar, white, 2 whole eggs, 8 drops extract almond. Place all on the fire till it reaches the boiling point. Remove and strain. Place in freezer and freeze. When nearly frozen, stir in the peach pulp. Give the freezer a few more turns to harden.

No. 276.

FRENCH VANILLA ICE-CREAM.

One quart of rich, sweet cream, ½ pound of granulated sugar, yolks of 6 eggs. Place the cream and sugar in a porcelain kettle on the fire, and allow them to come to a boil; strain immediately through a hair sieve, and having the eggs well beaten add them slowly to the cream and sugar while hot, at the same time stirring rapidly. Place them on the fire again and stir for a few minutes, then pour it into the freezer and flavor with 1 tablespoonful of vanilla, and freeze.

No. 277.

LEMON ICE-CREAM.

One quart of best cream, 8 ounces of pulverized sugar, 3 whole eggs, and a tablespoonful of the extract of lemon; place it on the fire, then immediately remove and strain. When cold place in freezer and freeze.

No 278.

CHOCOLATE TRANSPARENT ICING.

Melt 3 ounces of fine chocolate with a small quantity of water in a pan over the fire, stirring constantly until it becomes soft. Dilute this with ½ gill of syrup and work till perfectly smooth, then add to the boiled sugar as above.

Lightning Source UK Ltd.
Milton Keynes UK
UKHW010746271222
414464UK00004B/266